THE SCULPTURE OF
JOSÉ DE CREEFT

THE SCULPTURE OF
JOSÉ DE CREEFT

BY JULES CAMPOS

With a *Statement on Sculpture* by the Artist

KENNEDY GRAPHICS, INC. / DA CAPO PRESS, INC.
NEW YORK · 1972

Library of Congress Cataloging in Publication Data

De Creeft, José, 1884-
    The sculpture of José de Creeft.

    Bibliography: p.
    I. Campos, Jules.   II. Title.
NB237.D4C325   730′.92′4   77-166088
ISBN 0-306-70294-0

To EVA

CONTENTS

TORSO / 1906 / Clay
(First prize, Concours de Sculpture, Académie Julien, Paris, 1906)

JOSÉ DE CREEFT

WHEN my first book on José de Creeft was published twenty-five years ago, the major theme was the philosophy of direct carving as illustrated in his works. This philosophy is and always will be de Creeft's conviction concerning the art of sculpture. His search for artistic conceptions remains constantly in harmony with his respect for and knowledge of materials. Stones, wood, metals, ivory have been chiseled by his sapient hand, giving birth to a marvelous collection of carved works.

As this book illustrates, de Creeft has also mastered the techniques of casting in bronze, of modeling in clay, terra cotta, ceramic, of assemblage, construction, and combination of forms in all types of materials and media. But carving by the hammering hand is his first love.

The 283 works reproduced in this volume, created in a great variety of materials, are eloquent witness to de Creeft's vast command of his art. This is most apparent in his handling of stone, for stone starts by being the "adorable enemy" of the sculptor. He must attack it, dominate it, transform it into what he believes it should be, what he wants it to be. The stone is his enemy because it resists his will and often, during the sculptural process, offers surprises that are obstacles to his dearest aims.

Indeed, how almost insurmountable are the problems created by the geological caprices of serpentine, onyx, black marble, or ebony. When they were only stones or pieces of wood, de Creeft contemplated them with love. But his eye, his intellect, his turbulent emotions conceived in them a new fate. Under the energetic probing of his able hands, the stone has been vanquished, the work of art appears.

At the hand of the artist, granite is ennobled, lead finds a special glory, wood exhibits its ageless formations. The finished works acquire the impressive sense of strength and of increased volume so characteristic of his sculptural splendor.

CHILD OF SPAIN, José de Creeft was born in 1884 in Guadalajara, a little town situated on the banks of the Hanares River. Originally founded by the Romans, the city was later conquered by the Moors, who gave it the Arabic name for "Valley of Stones." By a strange destiny, this native of Guadalajara was to devote his life to admiring, loving, and restoring to its rightful glory that sculptural material.

De Creeft spent his childhood in Barcelona, his parents' native town. The premature death of José's father left the family destitute. Forced to earn his living at the age of thirteen, he entered the workshop of an *imagier*. This was the first of a series of apprenticeships which would make him a master of his art. In this studio filled with all sorts of wood, he felt his first artistic emotion as he observed the *imagier* carving with devotion and skill his saints and madonnas for the churches.

Later José worked in a foundry where the models of contemporary sculptors were cast and reproduced. There he learned the *cire-perdue* technique and the process of casting. His skill and ability attracted the interest of a foreman, who taught him new and improved methods. It was at this moment that José realized that craftsmanship was to be learned directly from the workers and not from distant masters; and these workers must have seemed exceptionally skillful, as they were able to reproduce with equal ability huge modern monuments and Cellini's subtly fashioned masterpieces.

At the age of sixteen, de Creeft moved to Madrid. There he continued his apprenticeship with Don Augustin Querol, at that time the Spanish Government's official sculptor. In Querol's studio, where most of the important public monuments of Spain were made, de Creeft became familiar with all phases of modeled sculpture technique. Yet the atmosphere of the studio seemed hostile to the young artist. His natural inclination toward independence, his desire to carve in the same way as the *imagier* of Barcelona left him unhappy with the routine tasks he had to perform. At the same time, frequent visits to the Prado and the Musée de Reproduction, where he sketched, served to refine de Creeft's artistic sensibility.

Poverty subsequently forced José to become a draftsman for the Madrid Administration of Bridges and Roads. This new work was interesting and valuable, as it taught him perspective and the discipline of precision drawing. His leisure time he devoted to free experiments in sculpture in his newly acquired studio on the Calle Espanoletto. Portraits of children were among his first works—only children were willing to pose for an unknown nineteen-year-old artist. Nevertheless, these portraits were very favorably received at the 1903 Exposición Extraordinaria organized in Madrid by El Circulo de Bellas Artes.

Despite this promising debut, de Creeft understood that he could improve his work only by studying in one of the great centers of art. He therefore decided to go to Paris, where he arrived in 1905 without means or connections, but with a burning enthusiasm. There he wandered in the museums, feeding on the strong emotions aroused by the sight of so many wonders. He soon realized that Paris would be his home. Wanting to begin serious study of sculpture, he visited Auguste Rodin, who advised him to enter an art school without delay: "With the experiences you have already acquired working in the studios and foundries of Spain, you have good chances of success in our Academies."

Encouraged by Rodin's advice, José entered the Académie Julien to complete his education as an artist. His creative ability soon won him recognition. The Académie Julien had instituted a competition for a figure in half-size. De Creeft rebelled against such constraint, determining instead to model a torso in natural proportions. Much to the disapproving surprise of the other students, and indifferent to all comments, he started and completed his *Torso* [facing page 1] in accordance with his own conception. By unanimous decision, the professors of the Académie Julien awarded him the first prize and congratulated him for having followed his idea through to the end without concession.

At that time, de Creeft lived with a friend from Madrid who had recently received the Prix de Rome. Together they set up a studio in the Batteau Lavoir on the Rue de Ravignan in Montmartre, a building in which Pablo Picasso, Juan Gris, and other progressive young artists also had their studios. This group gathered regularly in a small tavern nearby. De Creeft, whose ideas were clearly Academic, was frequently apt to take offense at the daring ideas of these artists. After his apprenticeships in Barcelona and Madrid, Rodin and Constantin Meunier represented for him the most daring expression in sculpture. Nevertheless, association with these young men, strongly dominated by Picasso, awakened in him doubts as to the value of Academic styles. The freedom and independence they proposed was an irresistible attraction for de Creeft.

In 1909 he exhibited his first portrait in bronze at the Salon des Artistes Français. As a result, he soon received many commissions for other portraits; and it was at this moment that he first experienced the conflict between *modeleur* and sculptor. He knew perfectly well how to make his clay models, but the Academies did not teach carving. Therefore, he had to entrust to *metteurs aux points* the actual reproduction in marble of his clay models. This made him realize that his education in the studios of other sculptors and in the Academies was woefully insufficient. Seeking advice from his professor at the Académie Julien, he was told that if he wanted to learn how to carve in stone, he should go to work at the Maison Greber, famous *metteurs aux points* of Paris. Here he made his first real contact with blocks of stone and wood, which ever afterward were to be for him the raw media of his sculpture. His first task was extremely difficult, calling for a scale reproduction, one-tenth larger than the original, of a head by Donatello. Noticing his skill on this project, Greber entrusted him with very delicate carvings, and for more than three years, de Creeft reproduced in stone the works of various sculptors modeled in clay.

The outbreak of World War I dealt terrible blows to art. De Creeft was forced to leave Greber for lack of work, but he did so without regret. He felt imprisoned by the servile process of reproducing clay models. Now that he knew the technique of carving in all of its intricacies, he desired to return to his own small studio where he could experiment freely and develop his own sculptural conceptions.

De Creeft began by modelling his portraits in clay and then reproducing them in stone, although relying only in part on *mise aux points*. But he was thoroughly unhappy with this redundant process. He fought constantly against the constraint imposed by the clay model, which denied expression to concepts developed as he worked on the stone, concepts suggested by the stone itself. Should he slavishly copy the pre-established model, whatever

[4]

sacrifice the material might suffer, or should he obey the dictates inherent in the block itself? De Creeft instinctively favored the will of the stone; but the Academies still gave precedence to an exact copy of the clay model. The conflict was crucial. De Creeft did not yet feel that ardent faith in his art which sculptors of all great eras have had. He wondered whether they had worked with such exuberance because they carved directly in the material. He came to believe so, and with resolution and courage, he followed Descartes' principle—he shook off all of the Academic doctrines he had previously accepted, he built "anew, from the very foundations, all the systems of his knowledge." Abandoning clay, that favorite of the masters of his time, he adopted what he defined as sculpture itself—direct carving.

From 1919 to 1928, de Creeft's works were exhibited in Paris at the Salon d'Automne, Salon des Tuileries, Salon des Artistes Indépendents, Société Nationale des Beaux Arts, Société d'Encouragement aux Arts, and elsewhere. His powerful forms at first occasioned only surprise, but the admiration both of critics and of the public soon followed. Plastic integrity and the absolute mastery of technique clearly placed de Creeft's works on a superior plane. Conceptions expressed through his impressive handling of masses gave evidence that a new contribution to sculpture was being made.

De Creeft came to the United States in 1929 and is now an American citizen. His first one-man American exhibition took place in Seattle a few months after his arrival, and exhibitions in New York and Chicago followed soon afterwards.

The atmosphere of freedom existing in the United States has been an important factor in the continuing development of de Creeft's sculpture. His use of direct carving has required sympathetic understanding devoid of prejudices created by established interests or by current ideas. From the time of his first exhibitions in this country, de Creeft has always been encouraged by discerning American art critics and by an understanding public.

In 1932, the New School for Social Research in New York organized a comprehensive exhibition of de Creeft's sculptures, and that same year he became a member of the New School faculty, teaching direct carving.

In the years since, de Creeft's sculpture has been exhibited constantly and purchased for a large number of leading collections. Honors and awards have been abundant. As early as 1923, the French government had nominated him an Officier de l'Instruction Publique. In 1942, he was awarded first prize in sculpture in the Metropolitan Museum of Art competition, *Artists for Victory*, for his *Maternity* [illustration 227]. In 1945 his portrait of Rachmaninoff [illustration 195] won the George D. Widener Memorial Gold Medal of the Pennsylvania Academy of Fine Arts, and a year later he was elected a fellow of the National Sculpture Society. Election as an Academician of the National Academy of Design followed in 1954, and selection to the fifty-member American Academy of Arts and Letters came in 1970.

Always active in the art world in America, de Creeft has been president of the Federation of Modern Painters and Sculptors, a founding member and vice-president of the Sculptors Guild, a vice-president of the Audubon Artists. As a member of countless juries determining awards to other sculptors, his contribution has been, and continues to be, important.

> *Sculptor, spurn the clay kneaded by the thumb; wrestle with carrara, with stones so hard and rare.*
>
> —Théophile Gautier

ART HAS FLUCTUATED between periods of high achievement and periods of decadence and sterility. At times, when the tide has been low, there have arisen men with courage and power to regenerate the greatness and integrity of their art. Sculptors from ancient Egypt, from archaic Greece, from the Roman and Gothic periods, and from the Renaissance not only were great artists, but great craftsmen as well. Sculpture for them meant carving in the block; *sculpere* meant possessing sufficient skill to impose one's will on the block. For these great masters, sculpture certainly did not mean modeling in clay and delegating to a craftsman the actual carving of the block. The sculptor was and is the man who carved.

Modeling and sculpture are in their very essence foreign to one another. What is perfect in clay might seem absurd in any other material. When modeling, one applies clay to clay, obtaining the final form by means of *adding* volumes to other volumes. But sculpture consists of disengaging material to reach a hidden form contained in the block. It is a process of subtraction, not of addition.

[6]

During the nineteenth and early-twentieth centuries, sculptors lost sight of this truth and the integrity of sculpture degenerated. As the artist drew further away from his ultimate material, he forgot the great traditions of his art. As a result, the work even of the great masters of the period remained short of perfection, invariably betraying its immediate derivation from originals in clay. The stone, as a precise mechanical reproduction of soft surfaces, seems to be lacking in solidity. One can see what is missing—the thousand nuances of the carver which no intermediary can replace without destroying the quality.

Fortunately, an intellectual movement which questioned this practice arose toward the end of the nineteenth century. "Sculptor, spurn the clay," exclaimed Théophile Gautier. Baudelaire affirmed that "in its finality sculpture is not meant to be a rival of modeling." Encyclopedias discerningly compared Michelangelo's brilliant skill to the laborious manipulations of modern sculptors:

> The practice of most modern sculptors is to do very little to the marble with their own hands: some, in fact, have never really learnt how to carve, and thus the finished statue is often very dull and lifeless in comparison with the clay model. Most of the great sculptors of the Middle Ages left little or nothing to be done by an assistant; Michelangelo especially did the whole of the carving with his own hands, and when beginning on a block of marble attacked it with such vigorous strokes of the hammer that large pieces of marble flew about in every direction.*
>
> *"Sculpture," Encyclopedia Britannica, 11th Edition (1911).

A practical reaction against modeling began to take shape among artists in Paris around the turn of the century. The sculptor Joseph Bernard was one of the first in his time to carve directly. After him came Matteo Hernandez, who carved animal figures in stone from living models. Then José de Creeft, breaking with all the principles established by his predecessors of the previous century and by his contemporaries, decided to abandon modeling in clay, that "soft and muddy" sculpture. The task of completing the revival of carved sculpture could only be undertaken by a great and vigorous artist. José de Creeft's talent and perseverance led him to wage and win the battle of direct carving.

In his evolution, de Creeft went through several stages. Definitely abandoning the model method taught in the Academies, he interested himself in the *taille classique*, the technique of Michelangelo, involving use of a small maquette in wax or plaster to help the artist arrive at the main lines of his work. But the maquette was all too confining. While carving, the block suggested to de Creeft new conceptions which were constantly at odds with the discipline imposed by the maquette. (Michelangelo, too, had felt such constraint, and by way of reaction he had carved several works in marble without use of a maquette.)

Later de Creeft devoted himself to carving *d'après nature*, using a living model. However, the model seemed to constitute yet another obstacle to his creative freedom, and he next tried carving from a series of drawings. Here, too, the bridle was felt; the composition still seemed to be excessively predetermined by the drawings. Unsatisfied with these attempts, stimulated by an instinct that directed him toward absolute freedom of expression, José de Creeft then discarded preparatory models and sketches, and began his marvellous struggles directly with the block. Thus the artist and his materials once again came to confront each other in a situation of complete freedom. Creation and execution became simultaneous.

De Creeft has always believed that the hand should obey the intellect, because the intellect conceives and the hand executes. However, there are situations where the intellect must accept suggestions from the hand. The materials for sculpture vary widely. Some, such as white marble or limestone, being uniform in consistency, are docile. For such materials, the intellectual conception is sovereign. But this is not true for certain granites, colored marbles, serpentines, and woods. These materials are not docile or neutral. They confront the sculptor with a will of their own, and he must respect their dictates and modify his conceptions accordingly. His work will only be at its best when he has succeeded in finding a harmonious solution which satisfies both his conception and the exigency of the block. Of course, stones and woods reveal their secrets only to those who love them and try to understand them.

In a relevant lecture on ethics given at the New School for Social Research, Jacques Maritain explained that every individual bears in himself "pre-moral dispositions" which could be defined as "general dispositions toward life." These dispositions exist in every child, and it is the responsibility of the sensitive teacher to discover them and to adapt his method of education to them.

Maritain added that "these pre-moral dispositions could be compared to the beauty of the material before being transformed by a sculptor."

In the field of sculpture, José de Creeft believes that each block of material possesses characteristics which the sculptor must grasp. These are "pre-sculptural" dispositions—the shape of the block, the grain, texture, color, the degree of hardness, and the like. It is the sculptor's task to harmonize his conception with these dispositions.

In his work, de Creeft demonstrates a clear respect for the natural proportions of the block. Indeed, because of his effort to conserve most of the original volume, many of his works seem to be larger when finished than the block from which they have been carved.

Beyond this respect for the proportions of the rough block, de Creeft's works illustrate skillful technical treatment of each material according to its grain, color, texture, and potential patina. Taken together, they are exemplary illustrations of the understanding treatment of an extraordinary variety of materials. De Creeft has worked in many kinds of wood, stone, marble, granite; in horn, ivory, plaster, clay, quartz, bronze, and lead, among other materials. He has employed an equally astonishing variety of techniques: direct carving, modeling, terra-cotta, bronze casting, plaster, ceramic, chased metal, and beaten lead, not to mention assemblage of chance materials. (Even stove pipes can give birth to a great creation if the artist understands their plastic destiny. See, for instance, illustration 277.)

From all of this—conception, sympathy toward materials, technique—the works emerge. They are marked by a remarkable simplification of line characteristic of de Creeft's interpretation of nature. Only the main sweep of the form is important. Details are secondary because they detract from the principal idea by drawing too much attention to themselves. All of de Creeft's works bespeak such simplification. Even his portraits are conceived only in a few broad lines which frame the whole composition. In this way, they become more than mere portraits; they transcend the element of resemblance and attain the status of inspired interpretations.

De Creeft early became interested in architectural sculpture. Like the artists of antiquity and the middle ages, he preferred to do his work right at the building. The sixteenth-century Fortaleza of the Island of Majorca has been entirely renovated with capitals [illustrations 268, 271, 272], doors, fountains [illustrations 273, 276], and stairs that de Creeft carved during a period of eighteen months in 1927, 1928, and 1929. During these months, he worked right in the courtyard, believing that architectural sculpture executed on the spot is superior to that made elsewhere, since the artist always has before him the appropriate proportions and the changing effects of light. As a result, de Creeft's works executed at the Fortaleza of Majorca are masterpieces of proportion and harmony. The capitals of the columns represent different animals: elephants, fishes, owls, rams, snakes, all forcefully stylized. The fountains, bursting with tremendous volume, were intentionally made conspicuous by the artist in order that they might be the natural center of the scenery.

Among de Creeft's other public sculpture, his carved *Poet* [illustration 59] contemplates Fairmount Park in Philadelphia, while his *Alice in Wonderland* [illustration 282] charms and stimulates the fantasy of visitors to New York's Central Park. *Alice* is never alone—children play around it, climb on it, hide under it, slide off it. Their activities prove how well José de Creeft knew the message of "Alice."

The works of a sculptor cannot be described, they must be seen. That is the point of view of this book. The illustrations bring into sharp focus the full scope of José de Creeft's achievement. As this is written, de Creeft is in his eighty-eighth year. It is safe to prophecy that he will have a strong and lasting influence on the future of sculpture.

JULES CAMPOS

ACKNOWLEDGEMENTS: I wish to extend my wholehearted thanks to the artist for helping me to obtain the pictures of his works and for providing the basic information upon which the book is based.
My sincere gratitude also to Edward Rambusch and David Rattner for their assistance in the translation of my manuscript, which was originally written in French.
To Lorrie Goulet de Creeft for her invaluable assistance in the preparation and completion of the volume.
To my daughter Flora for her kind help in reviewing the final text.
To James Barnett and Ricardo Amy for their dedicated work on the design and production of the work.
To Dr. Francis A. L'Esperance, Jr., for having made this work possible by restoring to me what Aristotle called "the most precious sense"—sight.

J.C.

STATEMENT ON SCULPTURE*

Everything that you discuss has a head and a tail. Some people pick the tail and others the head; most forget the body. It is the same when one speaks of art. Art cannot be explained—how can it when it arouses in man inexplicable feelings? You can discuss your ideas, your methods, your approach. But the art that you produce has to be seen; it must speak for itself.

What is sculpture for me?

It is an expression in a material of my ideas, my loves, and my philosophy. I use plastic form as a writer uses words. My feelings find release in form through my hammer and chisel. I never really set out to make a piece of "art," though I am sure my inner hope is that my sculpture will have such value. I work in a material to get the most out of it.

To be a sculptor one must like materials and manual labor. The more you work with the material, the more it becomes your friend. If you like stones and carve them, any stone will contain unlimited forms.

Stones for the sculptor can be seductive. The irregular ones mean the most. A rectangular stone, such as you find in the quarries, will probably say little to you unless you have gone there with a rigid, preconceived idea which needs a certain kind of marble or granite in which to execute it. This rarely happens to me. The conception I begin with is never rigid. I see a piece of stone and I have a desire to carve it. My ideas develop as I work, and as long as there is material, there is possibility for change. I am not slave to the stone, nor do I use a maquette.

A maquette is a small study for a piece intended to be made much larger. Its use is undoubtedly as old as the art of carving, and yet it is probably respon-

*Reprinted from Fernando Puma, ed., *Seven Arts 2* (New York: Doubleday, 1954) by permission of the estate of the editor.

[11]

sible for much of the bad sculpture in the world. To repeat yourself word for word, stroke for stroke, from the small to the large, usually means to lose the essential feeling somewhere in between. You impose upon the final piece an alien shape which does not arise from its natural qualities. Unless the maquette is simply a point of departure, it turns you into an artisan, a person putting in a day's labor, and the result is what one might expect.

There seems to be a growing interest in direct treatment of materials—a principle for which I have stood during the fifty-some years I have been carving. This attitude hardly existed when I began. In those days, everything was modeled in clay or plasticine and then cast into bronze or translated into stone at the commercial studios run by artisans. I myself spent a few years in such a studio in Paris, the Maison Greber, where I went with one idea in mind, to learn the processes. But my interest and belief in direct carving dates from an even earlier time. When I was sixteen, a group of Eskimos pitched their tents near Madrid. I discovered at their exhibit a group of carvers who made figures and motifs in ivory. I already had a little knowledge of carving, since at the age of thirteen I had passed some time as an apprentice to an *imagier* who made religious figures for the Church of Spain. This experience had not satisfied me because the figures were poorly conceived and were for the most part copies of seventeenth-century sculptures. But the Eskimos impressed me with their simplicity and their directness. With tiny pieces of ivory they made monumental sculptures—sculptures that had strength, power, and serenity, although they were less than hand-size. From this moment on, I became interested in all sculpture done in the same direct way.

Later, in Paris, where I went when I was nineteen to follow my art, I found everyone working in clay or plasticine, substances which have always seemed essentially dead to me. Clay has no will of its own—no resistance. It is like a person who says yes, yes, yes. There is nothing to overcome in it. It is soft and too quick to bend to your will. When you work in clay you create so quickly that you are apt to exhaust your emotion before you have perfected your idea. Clay has none of the inner "valor" of wood or stone or metal. The only live thing about a modeled form is its armature, which you cover up. Modeling exercises in school serve to give the student a greater awareness of the forms in nature, but one should remember always that modeling is exactly the opposite process from carving.

A sculpture, etymologically, is an object carved by the hand of man. Today, however, sculpture is the term loosely applied to all objects that represent an artist's expression of form in space. Many things are called sculpture which I do not think deserve the name, but there are others for which we shall have to find room within meaning of the term.

In any case, it is a question of who is doing it. If you are not a musician and you try to make music with casseroles and wooden spoons, you will only make noise and nonsense. A real musician with the same equipment may make pleasing sounds. It is an old saying that a sculptor with a hammer and a nail can make a masterpiece.

The contemporary sculptor has at his command hundreds of materials, and for the man who loves and appreciates them, not one is without its special character and beauty. It is actually not important what material you use, it is what you have to express; but without the love or affinity for some material in terms of the sculptor's craft, no creation is possible.

One of the most difficult and most important decisions the present-day sculptor has to make is selecting materials adaptable to his own ideas and personality. He may use one or combine several, he may compose a solo or a symphony. All doors are open—it is up to the individual.

Though most of my work has been in the form of direct carving in wood or stone, I have worked in and experimented with nearly all available materials, particularly beaten lead, hammered copper, and tin and metal construction. In 1925, for example, I used stovepipes, oil cans, bicycle tubes, insulated wire, and all kinds of odds and ends and pieces of junk to create my *Picador* [Illustration 277]. This piece was designed to show the inflated pride of those gendarmes of the bull ring as they ride their half-dead, martyrized horses. The rider carried a curtain-rod lance and the gored horse spilled tubes and wire from his belly. The *Picador* caused considerable comment in Paris when it was shown, and most of the discussion centered around its validity in terms of the materials employed. But the *Picador* and his materials were one; he could not have come into existence without them. In my enthusiasm, I did a number of similar pieces, including a *Maternity* and an *Ostrich*. It was a display of fireworks which nevertheless made sense.

I might have continued in this direction if I had not accepted a commission to carve some two hundred pieces for a fortress on the island of Majorca. During

[13]

the eighteen months I passed at that work, carving directly in the native stone, I reaffirmed my beliefs that to treat any material directly is the only truly creative approach and that only materials like wood and stone make possible the permanence and monumentality I have always sought. I experiment, but I always come back to these two materials, probably because of their naturalness and simplicity and inner "valor."

By no means do I intend to limit the sculptor in the materials he uses. Yet I would like to point out that it is a curious man indeed who thinks so little of himself, his life, and his art that he creates in a material with no real hope of permanence. Experimentation, yes—but its purpose after all is to find something worth finding and worth keeping.

Sculpture in permanent materials takes time to produce, as well as many years of prior experience in the crafts appropriate to such materials. There are no short cuts to permanence, just as there are no substitutes for integrity. The ambition to produce in quantity is dangerous because it deprives you of the enjoyment of being both a friend to your ideas and a friend to your materials. Materials have qualities which will speak to you if you listen.

I find, for example, that the use of the air hammer on stone disturbs my thoughts. I was once accused, while giving a demonstration in a museum, of using the tools of a caveman. I explained to my critic that the noise and speed of the machine came between me and the stone. I want to hear my thoughts and I want to hear what the stone says to me. Furthermore, I like the stone—otherwise, I would not carve it. The machine was invented to economize time and labor. Let the artist go slowly; he must give time and labor without counting.

Sculpture is the creation of three-dimensional form in space. In my opinion, the most fundamental principle required to obtain that end is the use of massive volume and contour. I cannot believe that sculpture is a mechanical toy, a feat of engineering, or a series of spaces in a material. It is the form you have given to the material itself.

There has been an attempt to reverse this logic, to try to use a material to indicate spatial form. I am not against experimentation which might broaden the concepts of sculpture, yet I feel that art must evoke an emotional response through its forms. The idea of space, it seems to me, is more intellectual than emotionally evocative. Empty space is always the same; but materials, which must exist in some form or other, vary infinitely—in volume and contour, in hardness or softness, in the way they take light, in color—in sum, in all the things which make us emotionally and sensually aware of them. Empty space is boring, but the material can be caressed, felt, and loved, as I believe a true piece of sculpture should be. Even in the attempts to form space, it is the material itself which draws our attention and which we appreciate for its own qualities.

May I repeat, a sculpture is the form you have given to the material—an object to be seen and touched and looked at from all sides and angles. As a unified form it ought to have what I call spiral movement—that continuity suggested by a contour which disappears and returns, giving the spectator the sense of its total existence in space. When this contour is successful (it can exist, of course, only in its relation to the volumes), the spectator will "know" that the piece exists in the round, regardless of the angle from which he views it. The meaning of the volumes as forms (not necessarily representative of natural objects) will come from their life in space and the way they suggest a feeling of unity.

In carving directly, the sculptor creates by releasing the forms he has seen hidden in the material, or perhaps it is better to say, the forms he has created in his mind and projected into the material. In either case, carving is the elimination of the excess material which covers the forms.

When I carve there is always a mutual relationship, a fluid and rhythmic exchange between myself and the material. This exchange does not stop—or rather, when it does stop, the piece is finished or at least carried as far as I can carry it at the time. A piece of sculpture is never finished. You stop when you put your hammer and chisel on the table. You do not put them down until the emotion which made you begin is exhausted. If you continue, you will drown your piece in the refinement of overwork.

As I have said before, the way one goes about fashioning his sculpture is an individual matter—manner and means—*chacun à son goût*. It is the same in all phases of art. The true artist is not a specialist limited to one way of expression. He never abandons his art; his whole life is oriented toward it. Like love, it is a passion that takes possession of him. Since his art depends solely on him, he will be egotistical. And because he is trying to be creative, which is in itself a demonstration of human aspiration, he must learn to accept and to be himself. This last is the real sign of his maturity.

No artist is a born master; he is born only with the soul of an artist. His development should be like a pyramid, broad-based and solid. I teach and encourage my students to carve directly because it provides strength through the discipline it requires and the satisfaction it offers in answering the challenge. It is a challenge that gives a solid beginning. One can find himself in the stone.

I realize and understand the disquiet existing among today's sculptors who wish to follow other roads than the one I have taken. I am not opposed to any school or movement in art. Every branch of the tree is an outgrowth of the trunk. Some pruning needs to be done, as always, but with time the weak branches will wither and fall of their own accord.

One of the weak branches is that which is termed "primitive art." Primitive art is impossible today. Everyone is sophisticated and has absorbed too much to recover the unconscious attitudes underlying this art. Sophisticated ignorance and ineptitude is, after all, immature—stupid. Everyone has an "age in art" differing from his real age, based upon his ability or inability to create forms open to his imagination.

The general public has always been more interested in craftsmanship than in the forms which art intends to express. Another weak branch of the tree is the sculpture which aims to serve this interest in "effects"—in surface manipulation for its own sake, in purposeful pre-aging and mutilation (the deceits of the antique dealer) and the general misuse of materials. Naturally the artist must know his craft, *mais vous devais le savoir cacher.*

On the other hand, there is a new anatomy which has discovered the value of forms in their own right. A wider understanding is that if you adapt nature you will come closer to it than if you copy nature. There is more interest in the direct treatment of materials, and the very existence of totally new ones has demanded new techniques to handle them.

And yet we appear to be in a period of pronounced dissonance. Never have the arts seemed more divergent. This might be interpreted as pointing to the instability of modern man. Perhaps the speed of the wheels of scientific progress leads the man of our age to abandon his idea of permanence as he vainly struggles to maintain his equilibrium in so dynamic an age. Yet it is more as if he were a cork in a whirlpool. He believes he is moving forward when in reality he is circling toward oblivion. The current is stronger the more he approaches the center; absorption comes nearer day by day.

The role of the artist has always been to express his beliefs and his feelings about life and to elevate mankind by demonstrating man's creative aspirations. He has expressed what he dreams as well as what he sees. I do not say that the artist must necessarily copy the surface of nature, though he cannot possibly alienate himself from the forms of nature, since they are all there if you look for them. As an artist, no matter how obscure or diverse his creation may appear, he is still a segment of nature itself.

Years ago I took a more orthodox view of art, but as time went on, my ideas changed. I have concluded that although much of what is done today is not entirely convincing, it nevertheless gives promise for the future. I see it as an embryonic beginning after a long and fallow period. I certainly cannot visualize the future of sculpture completely, but I can see that this art has broadened and today includes many new points of departure. Whether or not we accept any one of them will depend on our degree of understanding and the maturity of the artists we try to understand.

In my own work I find greater freedom than ever before! I see more each day. I would not want to close the door on anyone—nor on myself. To me, this is one of the most exciting periods in the long history of art. Since 1900, we have experienced changes and seed plantings as never before. Sculpture, for example, has delivered itself from the enslavements of the nineteenth century—from the compass, the pointing machine, rigid copying from the model, the pantograph. The chains and veils have been torn away. New freedoms based on solid concepts have revived what once appeared to be a dying art.

I believe that stone and metal will be the chief vehicles of sculptural expression in the future and that they will be handled directly. Their increased use, coupled with the artistic integrity necessary to treat them, can help to bring back the sense of stability we all long for.

It is my hope that the young sculptors will conserve the bridges connecting them with the sculptors of ancient times and that the roads they build in the future will be related to their origins. Not to be primitive, but to be genuine, and to convey with these ageless elements modern and universal thought.

José de Creeft

THE SCULPTURE OF
JOSÉ DE CREEFT

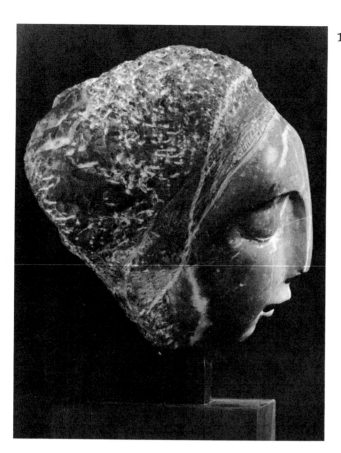

1. PAMELA / 1964 / Red Spanish Marble
Collection of Mrs. Virginia Gedney, New York, N.Y.

2. FRUFRU / 1966 / White Carrara Marble
Collection of Dr. and Mrs. Arthur E. Kahn, New York, N.Y.

3. OPULENCE / 1964 / White Georgia Marble
Collection of the Whitney Museum of American Art

4. GUATAMALA / 1965 / Black Belgian Granite
Collection of Mr. and Mrs. David Ross, New York, N.Y.

5.   KABUKI / 1964 / Green Serpentine Stone
Collection of Mrs. Lawrence K. Marshall, Cambridge, Mass.

6.   SLEEPER / 1955 / Black Diorite
Collection of Mr. and Mrs. Milton Nebenzohl, Great Neck, N.Y.

◄ 7. PASSION / 1964 / Black African Wonderstone
     Collection of Mr. and Mrs. George Farkas, New York, N.Y.

8. THE DREAM OF EVE / 1958 / Green Gneiss
    Collection of Dr. and Mrs. Arthur E. Kahn, New York, N.Y.

9. THE SECRET / 1966 / Green Gneiss
    Collection of Mr. and Mrs. William Kabbash, Greenwich, Conn.

10. SEATED WOMAN / 1921 / Portuguese Granite
Collection of the Artist (Courtesy of Kennedy Galleries)

11–12. REFLECTION / 1962 / Green Serpentine Stone
Collection of Mr. and Mrs. George Farkas, New York, N.Y.

13. PALOMA / 1964 / White Carrara Marble
Collection of J. Frederic Lohman, Ltd., New York, N.Y.

14. HEAD / 1965 / Brown Alabaster
Collection of Mr. Nathan Rothstein, Great Neck, N.Y.

15. TRANQUILITY / 1964 / Red Sandstone
Collection of Dr. and Mrs. Arthur E. Kahn, New York, N.Y.

16. UNIDAS / 1968 / White Carrara Marble
Collection of Mr. and Mrs. Jack Leason, New York, N.Y.

17. DREAM / 1964 / White Alabaster
Collection of Mrs. Jean Trotsky, Forty Fort, Pa.

18. UNE AME / 1944 / White Carrara Marble
*Collection of Mr. and Mrs. Milton Lowenthal,
New York, N.Y.*

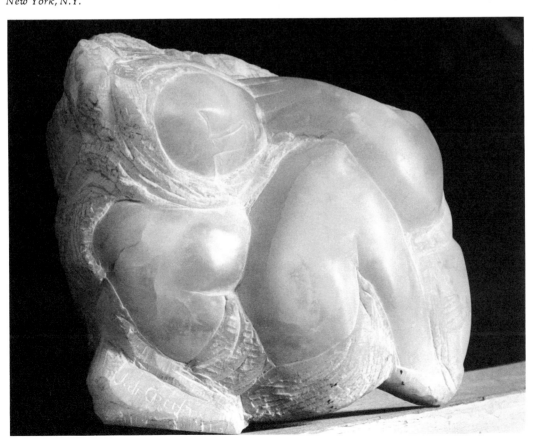

19. MATURITY / 1950 / French Limestone
Collection of Kennedy Galleries, New York, N.Y.
(Anonymous Award, Audubon Artists, 1954)

20. FIGURE / 1932 / Ivory Walrus Tooth
Private Collection

21. LILLIAN / 1960 / White Alabaster
Private Collection

22. FLAME / 1966 / White Marble
Collection of Mr. and Mrs. Louis Friedenthal, New York, N.Y.

23. CREPUSCULE / 1966 / Green Serpentine Stone
Collection of Mr. Harris J. Klein, Brooklyn, N.Y.

24. YOUNG GIRL / 1944 / Red Sandstone
Collection of Judge S. R. Levine, Peekskill, N.Y.

25. SLEEPING WOMAN / 1928 / Terra Cotta
Private Collection of the Artist

27. ACROBAT / 1955 / French Limestone
Collection of Mr. and Mrs. William Ginsberg, New York, N.Y.

◀26. CHRYSEIS / 1945 / Bluestone
Collection of Mr. and Mrs. Alfred Berman, New York, N.Y.

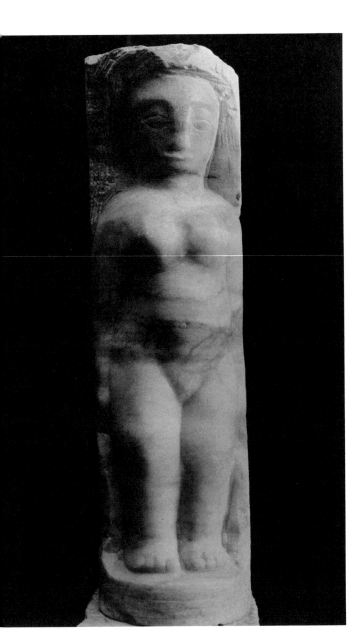

28. COLUMN FIGURE / 1958 / Pink Alabaster
Private Collection

29. BAMBINO / 1966 / Pink Georgia Marble
Collection of Mr. and Mrs. Fred Golden, Westport, Conn.

30. VOLUPTAS / 1938 / White Georgia Marble
Billy Rose Collection, Bezalel Museum, Jerusalem

33. NADADORA / 1966 / Limestone ▸
*Collection of Mr. and Mrs. Stephen Chodorov,
New Milford, Conn.*

31. PERUVIAN INDIAN / 1937 / Pink Tennessee Marble
Private Collection

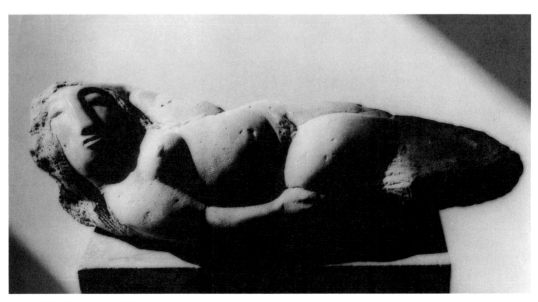

32. MAJA / 1958 / Green Sedimentary Stone
Collection of Mr. and Mrs. Henry Rubin, New York, N.Y.

34.   SIESTA / 1961 / White Carrara Marble
Collection of Mr. Joseph L. Brown, Oyster Bay, N.Y.

35. TRIPELAIRE / 1960 / Red Spanish Marble
Collection of Mrs. Shirley P. Halperine,
New York, N.Y.

36. SLEEPING WOMAN / 1960 / Limestone
Collection of Mr. Jerome Seigal, New York, N.Y.

37.   EMBRYONIC FORMS / 1957 / Green Serpentine Stone
Hirshhorn Museum and Sculpture Gardens, Smithsonian Institution

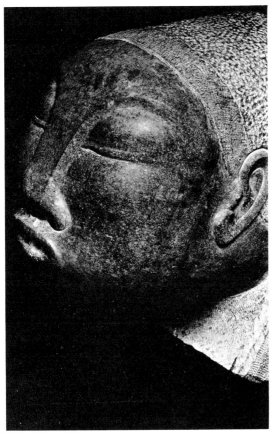

38. FONTAINE / 1929 / Pink Tennessee Marble
Collection of the Kirby Lane North Association, Rye, N.Y.

40. WINTER / 1963 / White Mahogany
Collection of Mr. and Mrs. Milton Goldhair,
Larchmont, N.Y.

39. STORM / 1964 / Brown Serpentine
Collection of Mrs. R. A. Hooker, New York, N.Y.

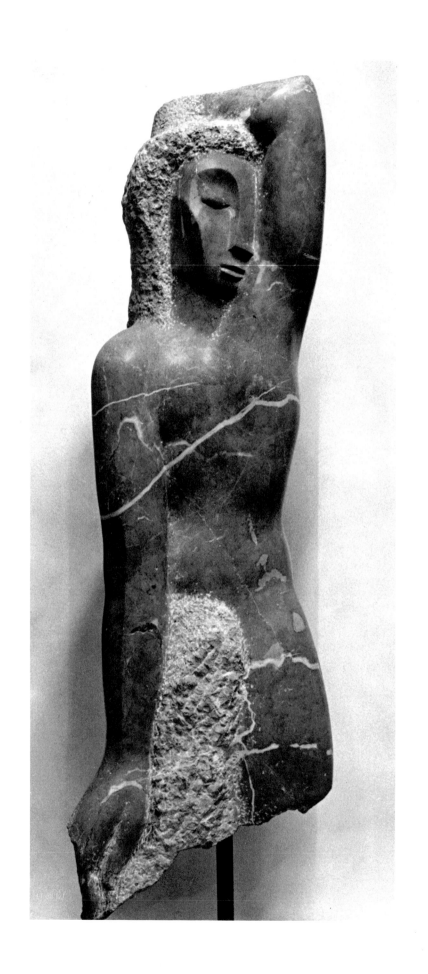

42. CLOUD / 1940 / Greenstone
Collection of the Whitney Museum of American Art

◄41. NEW BEING / 1967 / Red Spanish Marble
Collection of the Artist (Courtesy of Kennedy Galleries)

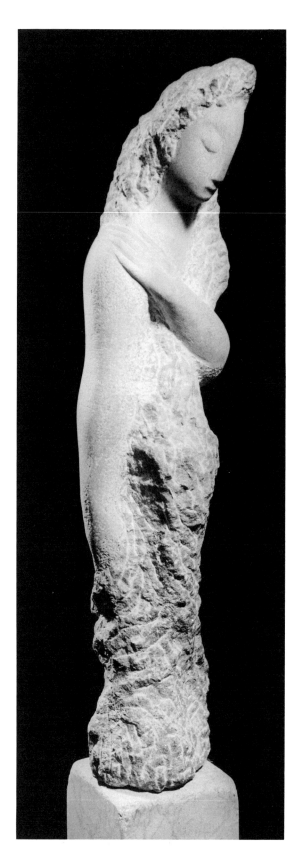

43. POESIE / 1960 / Pink Tennessee Marble
Collection of Margaret Wasserman Levy, Philadelphia, Pa.

44. ATENA / 1956 / White Marble
Collection of Miss Jane Owen, Dallas, Texas

45. CARYATID / 1958 / Green Serpentine Marble
Collection of Dr. Barnet Fine, Stamford, Conn.

46. IBERICA / 1938 / Black Porphyry
Collection of Mr. and Mrs. Milton Lowenthal, New York, N.Y.

47. THE HAND OF CREATION / 1967 /
White Carrara Marble
*Collection of the Art Students League,
New York, N.Y.*

48. ETOILE DE MER / 1942 / Pink Marble
*Collection of Mr. and Mrs. James Taylor Dunn,
Marine on St. Croix, Minn.*

49. OROUS / 1961 / White Marble
Collection of Dr. and Mrs. Myron Schwartz,
Bellemore, N.Y.

50. RIVER / 1954 / White Marble
Collection of Dr. Emil Arnold, New York, N.Y.

51. HAREM GIRL / 1963 / Green Gneiss
Collection of Mr. and Mrs. Sidney Jarcho, New York, N.Y.

52. LAMENTATION / 1961 / La Jolla Serpentine
Collection of Mrs. Eda Cohn, Ossining, N.Y.

53. EARTH / 1966 / Limestone
Collection of the Artist (Courtesy of Kennedy Galleries)

56. ESPANOLA / 1961 / Green Gneiss ▶
Private Collection

55. CHERUBINE / 1964 / Green Marble
Collection of Mr. Claude Bamberger, Teaneck, N.J.

54. NIOBE / 1958 / Green Serpentine Stone
Collection of Mrs. William Rand, New York, N.Y.

57.   EMERVEILLEMENT / 1941 / Green Serpentine Marble
Collection of the Metropolitan Museum of Art

58.   MAYA / 1939 / Black Belgian Granite ▶
Roland T. Murdock Collection,
Wichita Art Museum, Wichita, Kans.

59. THE POET / 1956 / Salisbury Pink Granite
Collection of the Fairmount Park Art Association, Philadelphia, Pa.

60. DREAM / 1961 / Pink Tennessee Marble
Collection of Lorrie Goulet de Creeft, New York, N.Y. (Therese and Edwin H. Richard
Memorial Prize, National Sculpture Society, 1969)

61. NEBULAE / 1950 / Purple Lithium
Collection of Mrs. Eda Cohn, Ossining, N.Y.

64. TETE / 1939 / Black Quartz
Collection of Mrs. Eda Cohn, Ossining, N.Y.

62. LA NINA / 1961 / Green Serpentine Marble
Collection of Mr. and Mrs. Henry Fischbach,
Purchase, N.Y.

63. MOUE / 1940 / Pink Quartz
Collection of Mr. Emil J. Arnold, New York, N.Y.

65.   LORRAINE / 1948 / Caen Stone
Collection of Lorrie Goulet de Creeft, New York, N.Y.

66. IBIZA / 1954 / Pink Granite
Collection of Dr. Robert Dickes, Brooklyn, N.Y.

67. EMBRACE / 1944 / Sienna Marble
Collection of Dr. and Mrs. James Rudel,
New York, N.Y.

68. OFFERING / 1961 / White Carrara Marble
Collection of Mr. and Mrs. William Ginsberg, New York, N.Y.

69. HEAD / 1961 / Red Slate
Collection of Mr. and Mrs. Lawrence Elow, Scarsdale, N.Y.

70. VISION / 1954 / Pink Tennessee Marble ▶
Collection of Mr. and Mrs. Robert Greenes, Scarsdale, N.Y.

◄ 71.   FLORA / 1968 / White Alabaster
         Collection of Dr. and Mrs. Dennis Cornfield, New York, N.Y.

72.   NIMBUS / 1961 / White Alabaster
       Collection of Mr. and Mrs. Henry Rubin, New York, N.Y.

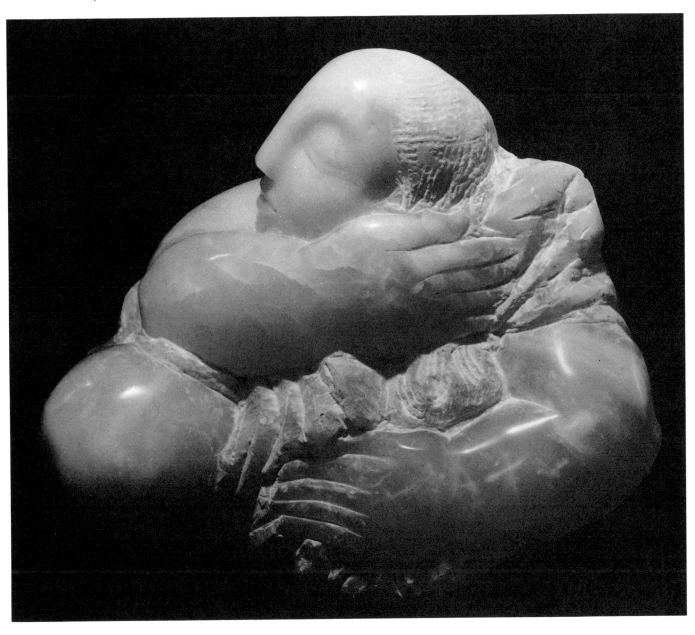

73. JEUNESSE / 1961 / White Alabaster
Collection of Mrs. R. Lawrence, Great Neck, N.Y.

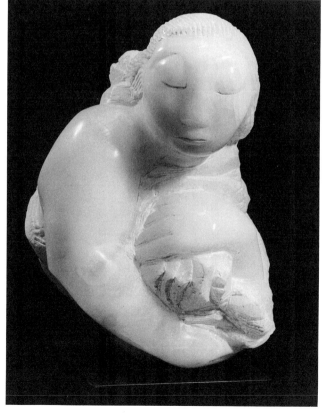

74. NIMBUS / 1961 / White Alabaster
Private Collection

75. ULYSSES / 1966 / White Alabaster
Collection of Mr. Ivin Brenner, New York, N.Y.

76. MUSE / 1954 / Russian Alabaster
Private Collection

77.   OPHELIA / 1949 / White Alabaster
Collection of Mr. and Mrs. Louis Friedenthal, New York, N.Y.

78.   FLORENTINE / 1961 / White Onyx ▶
Collection of Mr. and Mrs. Monroe Mark, New York, N.Y.

79.   NYMPH AND SATYR / 1961 / Botticine Marble
Collection of Mr. Harold Uris, New York, N.Y.

80. LA DAME DE PIQUE / 1940 / Limestone
Collection of Mr. and Mrs. Eugene Dluzynski, Jr.,
New York, N.Y.

81. THE DREAM / 1958 / Yellow Sienna Marble
Collection of the National Academy of Design, New York, N.Y.

82.   REPOSE / 1951 / Pink Tennessee Marble
Collection of Mrs. Alexander C. Speyer, Pittsburgh, Pa.

83.　LOVERS / 1940 / Limestone
Collection of the Artist (Courtesy of Kennedy Galleries)

84.　MONKEY / 1961 / Yellow Sienna Marble
Collection of Mrs. Louis Walker, New York, N.Y.

85.　MONKEY / 1942 / Green Serpentine Marble
Collection of Mrs. Charlotte Devree, New York, N.Y.

87.   PORTRAIT OF VALERIE DELACORTE / 1960 / Plaster for bronze
Collection of Mr. and Mrs. George T. Delacorte, New York, N.Y.

86.   DANCER / 1955 / Green Fieldstone
Collection of Dr. Theodore J. Edlich, New York, N.Y.

89. SPRING / 1940 / Pink Majorcan Marble
Collection of Mr. and Mrs. Owen Skelton, Palm Beach, Fla.

◄ 88. LA PENSEE / 1961 / White Georgia Marble
Private Collection

90. THE VEIL / 1958 / White Marble
Collection of Mrs. Paula Caro, New York, N.Y.

91. INCA / 1964 / Red Spanish Marble
Collection of Mrs. John O. Ross, New York, N.Y.

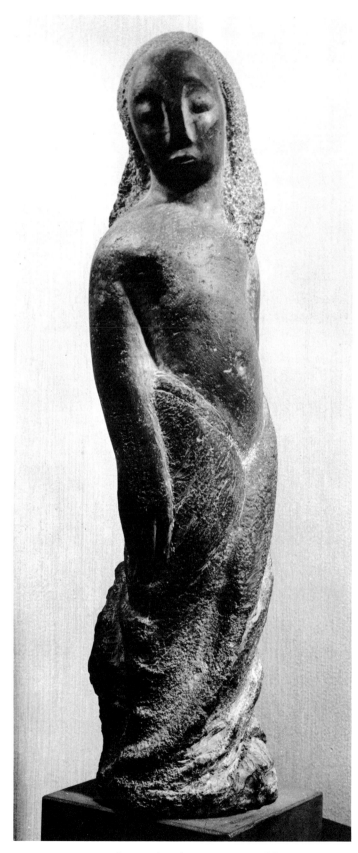

92.   INTIMACY / 1960 / Red Majorcan Marble
Collection of Mr. and Mrs. Sidney Jarcho, New York, N.Y.

94. SIAMORA / 1929 / Red Spanish Marble ▶
Collection of the Artist (Courtesy of Kennedy Galleries)

93. ANNA / 1967 / White Georgia Marble
Collection of Dr. and Mrs. Arthur E. Kahn, New York, N.Y.

95. GROUPE DES FEMMES / 1934 / Caen Stone
Collection of the Norton Art Gallery, West Palm Beach, Fla.

96. REVERIE / 1959 / White Carrara Marble ▶
Collection of Mr. and Mrs. Louis Friedenthal,
New York, N.Y.

97. ACQUATIC / 1964 / Green Serpentine Stone
Collection of Mr. and Mrs. Arthur Horowitz,
Miami Beach, Fla.

98. DANCE / 1961 / Green Gneiss
Collection of Mr. and Mrs. Fred Fields, Princeton, N.J.

99.   VEDAS / 1965 / Red Spanish Marble
Collection of Mr. and Mrs. Jesse Thaler, Fort Lauderdale, Fla.

101. CACTUS / 1938 / Greenstone
Collection of the Seattle Art Museum

100. FAWN / 1964 / Gray Granite
Collection of Dr. Lucille Blum, New York, N.Y.

102. SOLEIL / 1960 / Gray Marble
*Collection of Judge and Mrs. Abraham Gellinoff,
New York, N.Y.*

103. JUDITH / 1955 / Red Spanish Marble
*Collection of Mr. and Mrs. Walter Jacobson,
New York, N.Y.*

104. BOUQUET OF LOVE / 1971 / White Marble
Collection of the Artist (Courtesy of Kennedy Galleries)

105.   SOUCI / 1968 / Bronze (first cast)
Collection of the Greer Gallery, New York, N.Y.

107. GUARDIAN ANGEL / 1960 / Black Belgian Marble
Collection of Mr. James Boslow, Staten Island, N.Y.

106. NEGRA SUM SED FORMOSA / 1942 /
Black Marble
Private Collection

109.   BONITA / 1961 / Brown Steatite
Collection of Mr. and Mrs. S. J. Yannacci, Plainview, N.Y.

◄ 108.   JUANITO / 1945 / Green Serpentine Marble
Collection of the Sheldon Art Gallery,
University of Nebraska, Lincoln, Nebr.

110. RONDA / 1964 / Sandstone
Collection of Mr. and Mrs. Henry Rubin, New York, N.Y.

111. BAIGNEUSE / 1961 / Variegated Italian Marble
Collection of Mrs. Augusta Jacobson, New York, N.Y.

113. HEAD / 1965 / Black Belgian Marble
Collection of Dr. Ben Yasinow

112. CASTANETTAS / 1964 / Walnut
*Collection of Mr. and Mrs. Eugene Dluzynski, Jr.,
New York, N.Y.*

115. PRINTEMPS / 1958 / Brown Limestone
Collection of Judge S. R. Levine, Peekskill, N.Y.

114. JAVANESE / 1938 / Moroccan Onyx
Collection of Mrs. T. E. Hanley, Boston, Mass.

116.   HEAD / 1965 / Green Steatite
Senator William Benton Collection, New York, N.Y.

117.   SPIRIT OF THE FOREST / 1968 / Petrified Wood
Collection of Dr. and Mrs. Arthur E. Kahn, New York, N.Y.

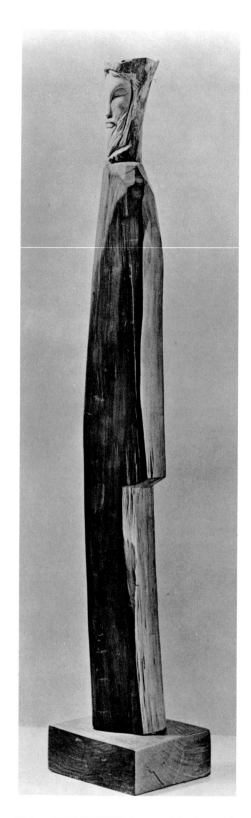

118.   THE JUDGE / 1933 / Cedar and Bone
Collection of Mrs. Eda Cohn, Ossining, N.Y.

119.   DAVID / 1968 / White Georgia Marble ▶
Collection of the Artist
(Courtesy of Kennedy Galleries)

120. HOBO / 1950 / Green Serpentine Stone
Private Collection

121. PROPHET / 1966 / Red Slate
Collection of Mr. and Mrs. Medwin B. Jeffer, Great Neck, N.Y.

122. JOSEPH / 1967 / Greenstone
Collection of the Greer Gallery,
New York, N.Y.

123. SHELTER / 1945 / Green Lithium
Collection of Georgette Passedoit, Paris

124. CREATURE / 1964 / Variegated Italian Marbl
Private Collection

125. DRAWING ON OBSIDIUM / 1964 /
Mexican Obsidium
Collection of the Artist (Courtesy of Kennedy Gallerie

126.   ATLANTIS / 1945 / Green Serpentine Marble
Collection of Indiana University of Pennsylvania, Indiana, Pa.

◄ 127. HEAD / 1965 / Green Serpentine Marble
Collection of Mr. and Mrs. Henry Wright, New York, N.Y.

129. CLAIR DE LUNE / 1964 / Green Steatite
Collection of Mr. W. Primoff, New York, N.Y.

128. PUREZA / 1958 / Russian Alabaster
Collection of Mrs. Lillian Sapirstein, New York, N.Y.

131. ECUADOR / 1923 / Black Belgian Granite
Collection of Mrs. Claire Nossiter, New York, N.Y.

130. CARAVELLE / 1964 / Limestone
Collection of Mr. and Mrs. Jack Leason, New York, N.Y.

132. FEMME ASSISE / 1938 / Greenstone
Hirshhorn Museum and Sculpture Gardens,
Smithsonian Institution

133. SOMNAMBULE / 1941 / Greenstone
Collection of Mrs. Elizabeth Payne Merris, Westport, Conn.

134. SKETCH / 1936 / Terra Cotta
      Collection of Lorrie Goulet de Creeft, New York, N.Y.

135. SKETCH / 1929 / Terra Cotta
      *Collection of Mr. and Mrs. Eugene Dluzynski, Jr.,
      New York, N.Y.*

136. FIGURE / 1930 / Terra Cotta
      Private Collection of the Artist

137. KNEELING FIGURE /
      1932 / Terra Cotta
      Collection of Mr. Rowland Burdon,
      Boston, Mass.

138. FIGURE / 1930 / Terra Cotta
      Collection of Mr. Max Jimenez

139. CONTINUITE / 1958 / Pink Georgia Marble
Collection of the Sara Roby Foundation, New York, N.Y.

140. FEMME A LA MAIN / 1958 / White Carrara Marble
Collection of Mrs. Clara Binswanger, New York, N.Y.

141.   AMA / 1964 / Red Sandstone
Private Collection

142.   SEATED FIGURE / 1965 / Pink Sandstone
Collection of Mr. and Mrs. Louis Bender,
Harrison, N.Y.

144. HELLENIC HEAD / 1932 / French Limestone
Collection of the Seattle Art Museum

145. MEDUSA / 1941 / White Carrara Marble
Collection of Mrs. Lillian Landis Gussow, New York, N.Y.

◄143. ROSA DE GRANADA / 1921 /
Black Belgian Marble
Collection of the Artist (Courtesy of Kennedy Galleries)

◄ 146. ASCENT / 1949 / Limestone
Collection of Mrs. Eda Cohn, Ossining, N.Y.

147. CREATIVE FORM / 1928 / Bois d'Orme
Collection of Lorrie Goulet de Creeft, New York, N.Y.

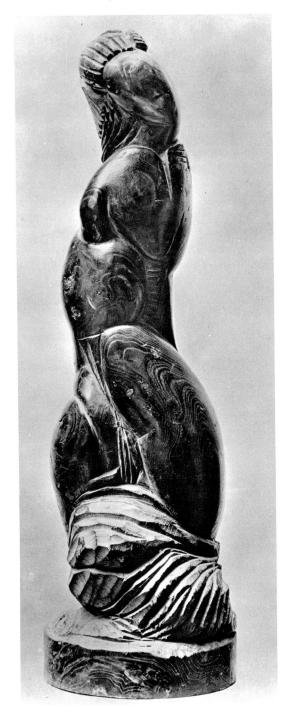

148. ANNUNCIATION / 1943 / Red Sandstone
Collection of the Artist (Courtesy of Kennedy Galleries)

150. NOVA / 1964 / Green Serpentine Stone
Collection of Tirca-Karlis, Provincetown, Mass.

151. FETICHE / 1916 / Green Serpentine Marble
Hirshhorn Museum and Sculpture Gardens,
Smithsonian Institution

◄ 149. PELEGRINO / 1958 / Green Steatite
Collection of Mr. A. L. Waintrob, New York, N.Y.

152.   ANGELITO / 1968 / Green Serpentine Marble
Collection of the Greer Gallery, New York, N.Y.

153. VICTOIRE / 1964 / Green Serpentine Marble
Collection of Dr. Anne Steinman, New York, N.Y.

154. SISTERS / 1963 / Green Serpentine Marble
Collection of Mr. and Mrs. H. R. Sheppard,
New Canaan, Conn.

155. JOHN / 1963 / Fieldstone
Collection of Mrs. Kurt Enoch, Willow County, N.Y.

156.   JOVEN / 1961 / Black Belgian Granite
Collection of Judge S. R. Levine, Peekskill, N.Y.

157.   PATRIARCH / 1967 / Brown Serpentine Marble
Collection of Mr. George Hanson, New York, N.Y.

158.   OFRENDA / 1966 / Brown Alabaster
Collection of Judge S. R. Levine, Peekskill, N.Y.

159.　MEDITERRANEAN GIRL / 1933 /
French Limestone
*Roland Murdock Collection, Wichita Art Museum,
Wichita, Kans.*

160.　FAUNA / 1940 / Caen Stone
*Collection of the Norton Gallery of Art,
West Palm Beach, Fla.*

161. ENIGMA / 1916 / Black Belgian Granite
Collection of Mr. and Mrs. Alfred Van Loen, Huntington Station, N.Y.

163. ASCETIC / 1964 / Fieldstone
Collection of Mrs. Jean Trotsky, Forty Fort, Pa.

164. LE GRAND SEMITE / 1938 / Red Slate
Collection of Mr. and Mrs. Norman Blankman, Sandspoint, N.Y.

162. NOAH / 1966 / Red Slate
Collection of Dr. and Mrs. Herbert Spasser, New York, N.Y.

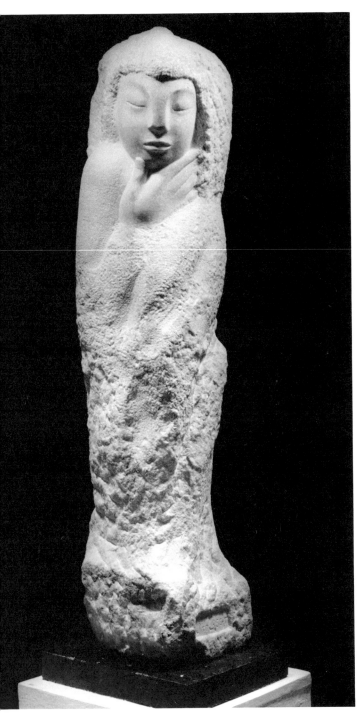

167. SERENITY / 1964 / White Carrara Marble ▶
Private Collection

166. SULKING WOMAN / 1944 / Chauvigny Stone
Hirshhorn Museum and Sculpture Gardens, Smithsonian Institution

165. MUSE / 1959 / White Georgia Marble
Collection of the Artist (Courtesy of Kennedy Galleries)

169. ANIMAL / 1950 / Brown Serpentine Marble
Collection of the Philadelphia Museum of Art

170. SLEEPING FOX / 1959 / Fieldstone
Private Collection

171. MONKEY / 1963 / Green Serpentine Marble
Collection of Dr. and Mrs. Arthur E. Kahn, New York, N.Y.

◄ 168. MONKEY / 1954 / Brown Serpentine Marble
Hirshhorn Museum and Sculpture Gardens, Smithsonian Institution

172. RECLINING CAT / 1950 / Black Marble
Private Collection
Bronze (first cast): Collection of Mr. and Mrs. William de Creeft, Homer, Alaska

174. GATO / 1961 / Green Serpentine Marble
Collection of Mrs. Celia Friedman, New York, N.Y.

173. CAT / 1958 / Red Marble
Collection of Mrs. Daisy Shapiro, White Plains, N.Y.

175. TIGEY / 1966 / Bresche Marble
Collection of Miss Cecile Singer, New York, N.Y.

176. AUX AGUETS / 1945 / White Marble
Formerly Collection of Mr. Billy Rose

177. SUNSET / 1942 / Red Marble
      Collection of Dr. Barnet Fine, Stamford, Conn.

178. LA NUIT / 1941 / White Carrara Marble
      Collection of Mr. Nathaniel Saltonstall, Boston, Mass.

179. AURORA / 1943 / Tennessee Marble ▶
      Collection of Eva Campos

180. CAPRICCIO / 1944 / Brown Coralline Marble
Formerly Collection International Business Machines Corporation

181. GROUP / 1938 / Pink Sandstone
Private Collection

182. ENTWINED FIGURES / 1936 / Green Serpentine Marble
Private Collection

183. PORTRAIT DU PEINTRE WALKOWITZ / 1943 / French Limestone
Private Collection

184. SEGUIDILLAS / 1940 / Greenstone
Collection of Dr. Theodore J. Edlich, New York, N.Y.

185. JEUNE NARCISSE / 1936 / Moroccan Onyx
Collection of Mr. Ian Woodner, New York, N.Y.

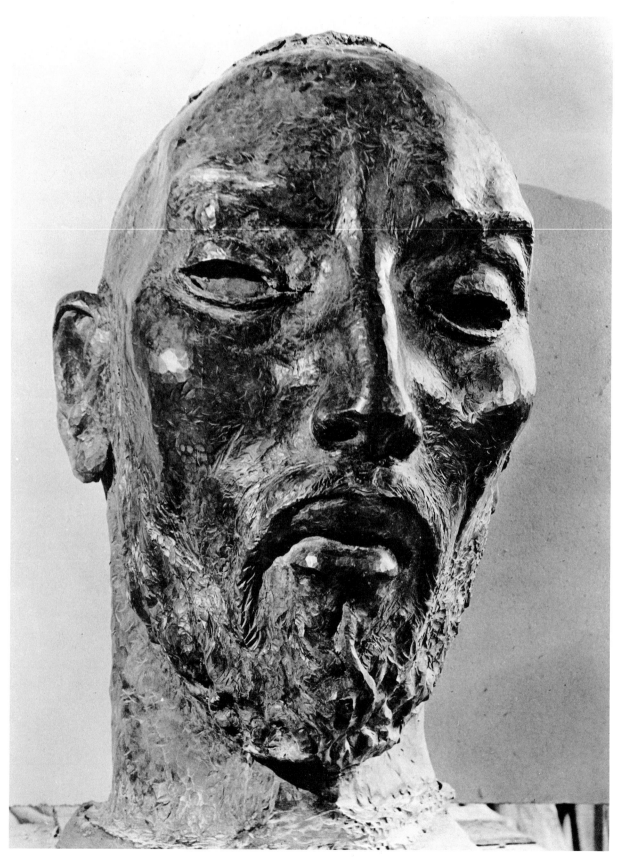

186.   HIMALAYA / 1942 / Beaten Lead
Collection of the Whitney Museum of American Art

187. MASK / 1958 / Hammered Silver
Collection of the Artist
(Courtesy of Kennedy Galleries)

188. SILENCE / 1963 / Beaten Lead
Collection of Mr. and Mrs. George T. Delacorte,
New York, N.Y.

189. DANCING CHILDREN / 1961 / Beaten Lead
Collection of the Artist (Courtesy of Kennedy Galleries)

190. DANTE / 1963 / Beaten Lead
Collection of the Artist (Courtesy of Kennedy Galleries)

191.   MADRELLIENE / 1963 / Beaten Lead
Collection of Mrs. Hal Goodman, New York, N.Y.

192.   THE APOSTLE / 1963 / Hammered Copper
Collection of the Artist (Courtesy of Kennedy Galleries)

193.   SEMITIC HEAD / 1936 / Beaten Lead
Collection of the Brooklyn Museum

194.   SATURNIA / 1939 / Beaten Lead
Collection of the Museum of Modern Art, New York, N.Y.

195. RACHMANINOFF / 1943 / Beaten Lead
Collection of the Pennsylvania Academy of Fine Arts,
Philadelphia, Pa.
(George D. Widener Memorial Gold Medal, 1945)

196. ESCLAVE / 1936 / Beaten Lead
Collection of the Artist (Courtesy of Kennedy Galleries)

197. YOUNG MOSES / 1929 / Beaten Lead
Collection of Mrs. T. E. Hanley, Boston, Mass.

198. SARITA / 1963 / Bronze
   Collection of Mr. Ramon Aspillaga, Lima, Peru

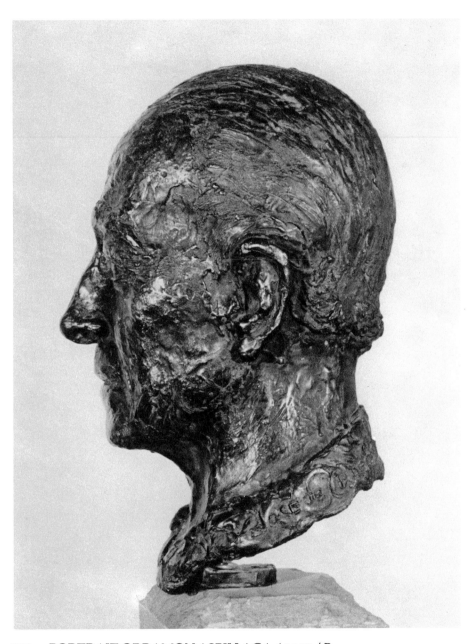

199. PORTRAIT OF RAMON ASPILLAGA / 1963 / Bronze
Collection of Mr. Ramon Aspillaga, Lima, Peru

200. MARGUERITE / 1918 / Bronze
Private Collection of the Artist

201.   LA SARRASINE / 1940 / Caen Stone
Private Collection

202. PORTRAIT / 1928 / Chiselled Lead
Collection of Muriel Mullins, Brooklyn, N.Y.

203. ROBERT / 1965 / Bronze
Collection of Mr. and Mrs. Alfred Shasha, Scarsdale, N.Y.

204. MEDICAL SCIENCE: THE GIFT OF HEALTH TO MANKIND / 1967 / Bronze
Collection of the Public Health Laboratory, Bellevue Hospital, New York, N.Y.

205. HEAD OF A BABY / 1958 / Beaten Lead
Private Collection

206. HARVEST / 1950 / Bronze
Collection of the Sheldon Art Gallery,
University of Nebraska, Lincoln, Nebr.

207. RECLINING NUDE / 1938 / Beaten Lead
Collection of Mrs. Eda Cohn, Ossining, N.Y.

208.   LES ADIEUX / 1941 / Beaten Lead
Collection of the Artist (Courtesy of Kennedy Galleries)

209. SELF-PORTRAIT / 1962 / Unique Bronze
Collection of Lorrie Goulet de Creeft, New York, N.Y.

210.   BERNARD SHAW / 1953 / Beaten Lead
Collection of Mr. and Mrs. Joseph Ternbach, Forest Hills, N.Y.

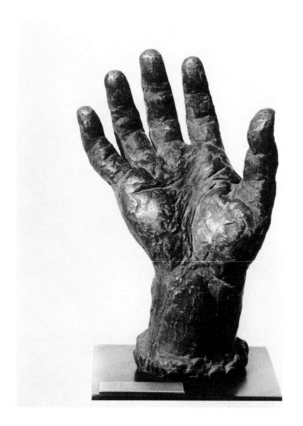

211. PORTRAIT HAND OF
DR. MERENDINO / 1964 / Bronze
*Collection of Dr. K. Alvin Merendino,
Seattle, Wash.*

212. FIGURE / 1950 / Bronze
*Collection of Mr. Stephen Schwartz,
New York, N.Y. (first cast);
collection of Mr. Ricardo Amy,
New York, N.Y. (second cast)*

213. KNEELING WOMAN / 1961 / Bronze
Private Collection

214. ORACLE / 1968 / Unique Bronze
Collection of the Artist (Courtesy of Kennedy Galleries)

215.   LES DEUX AMIS / 1941 / Beaten Lead
Collection of the Norton Gallery of Art, West Palm Beach, Fla.

216. NUDE / 1952 / Hammered Silver
Collection of Mr. Oliver Baker, New York, N.Y.

217. ORCHIDEE / 1919 / Chased Lead
Collection of the Artist (Courtesy of Kennedy Galleries)
Bronze: Collection of the Greer Gallery, New York, N.Y. (first and second casts)
collection of Lorrie Goulet de Creeft, New York, N.Y. (third cast)

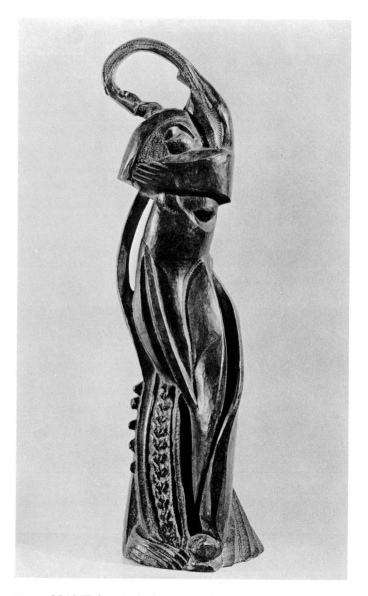

218. LIANE / 1927 / Chased Lead
Collection of Mr. and Mrs. Robert O'Knefski, Glen Head, N.Y.

219. PORTRAIT DU POETE VALLEJO / 1926 / Chased Lead
Collection of Mr. Lester Wolfe, New York, N.Y.

220. THE BEAUTY / 1963 / Unique Bronze
Collection of the Artist (Courtesy of Kennedy Galleries)

221. THE LUTE PLAYER / 1965 / Unique Bronze
Collection of Lorrie Goulet de Creeft, New York, N.Y.

222. MOSES / 1963 / Unique Bronze
Collection of Mr. Lewis Rowan, Great Neck, N.Y.

223. NIGHT / 1950 / Bronze
Collection of Mr. and Mrs. Louis Friedenthal, New York, N.Y. (first cast);
collection of Dr. and Mrs. Milton Goldstein, Scarsdale, N.Y. (second cast);
collection of Mr. and Mrs. Robert Kipniss, Brooklyn, N.Y. (third cast)

224. YOUNG GIRL / 1958 / White Georgia Marble
Collection of Mr. R. Lawrence, Great Neck, N.Y.

225. AZAIDE / 1957 / Green Sandstone
Collection of Dr. Edith Sheppard, Meadowbrook, Pa.

226.   LES ESCLAVES / 1944 / Green Serpentine Stone
Collection of the Munson-Williams-Proctor Institute, Utica, N.Y.

228. LE POILU / 1921 / Granite du Puy-de-Dôme
Saugues, France

◄ 227. MATERNITY / 1918 / Vosges Granite
*Collection of the Metropolitan Museum of Art (First Prize in Sculpture,
Artists for Victory, 1942)*

229.   DANCER / 1954 / Chestnut
Hirshhorn Museum and Sculpture Gardens, Smithsonian Institution

230.   STANDING FIGURE / 1939 / Georgia Pine
Collection of the Artist (Courtesy of Kennedy Galleries)

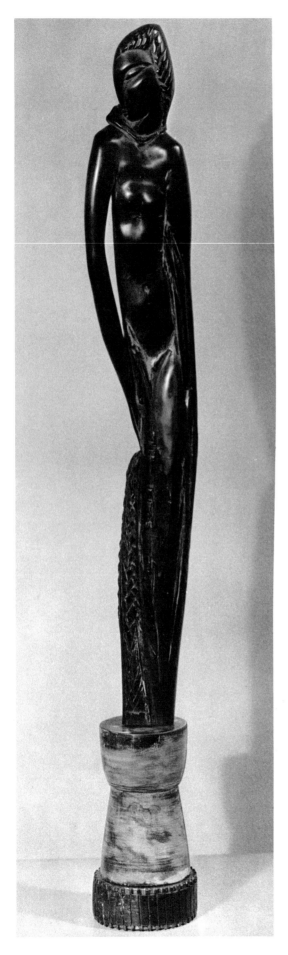

232. THE KNIFE / 1959 / Snakewood
Collection of Lorrie Goulet de Creeft, New York, N.Y.

231. BLACK LILY / 1929 / Ebony
Private Collection

233. BASQUE / 1961 / Snakewood
Collection of the Artist (Courtesy of Kennedy Galleries)

234. MADONNA / 1938 / Ivory
Collection of Mrs. T. E. Hanley, Boston, Mass.

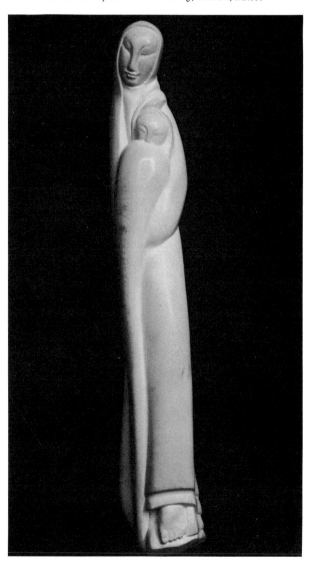

235. MASQUE / 1928 / Ceramic
Private Collection

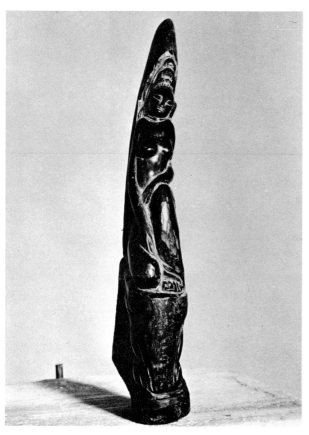

236. CEYLON / 1925 / Bull's Horn
Collection of the Artist (Courtesy of Kennedy Galleries)

237. CORDOVA / 1920 / Semi-Precious Pink Stone
Collection of Lorrie Goulet de Creeft, New York, N.Y.

238. FIGURE / 1929 / Snakewood
Collection of Mrs. Eda Cohn, Ossining, N.Y.

239. PHILOSOPHIE / 1958 / Wood and Stone
*Collection of Mr. and Mrs. Louis Baker,
Greenwich, Conn.*

240. FIGURE / 1952 / Ironwood
Private Collection

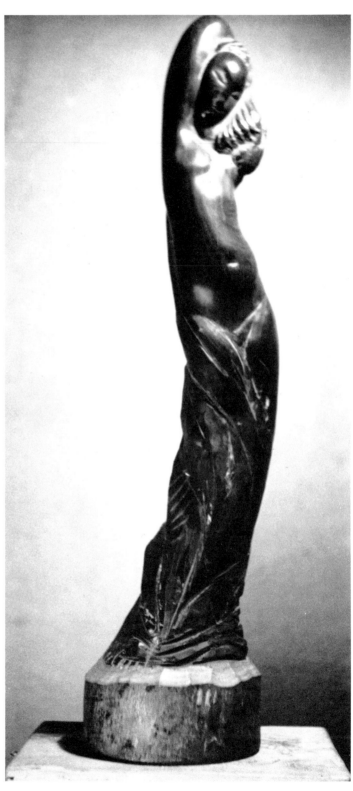

241. THE LORELEI / 1938 / Lignum Vitae
Collection of Mr. and Mrs. Robert Lubell

242.   CARYATID / 1921 / Ebony
Collection of Mr. Gordon Howe,
New York, N.Y.

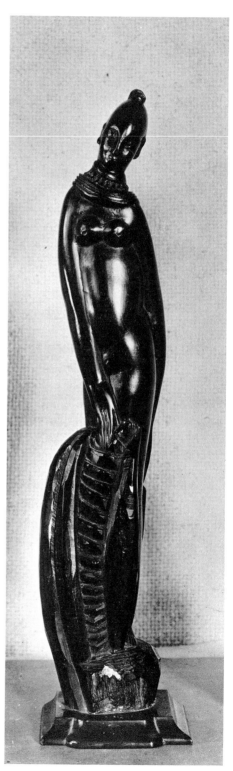

243.   AMAZON / 1921 / Ebony
Collection of Dr. Robert Pfeffer,
New York, N.Y.

244.   SUZANNE / 1921 / Ebony
Hirshhorn Museum and Sculpture Gardens,
Smithsonian Institution

245.   SLAVE GIRL / 1921 / Ebony
Collection of Mr. and Mrs. Robert Ward,
Chicago, Ill.

247. POLENSIA / 1922 / Bois d'Indochine
*Collection of Dr. and Mrs. Louis Small,
Passaic, N.J.*

246. SALAMMBO / 1939 / Georgia Pine
Collection of Eva Campos

249.   ABSTRACT / 1928 / Olivewood
Collection of Mr. and Mrs. Edward Marks,
Leesburgh, Va.

248.   PEACE / 1930 / Olivewood
Collection of Mr. and Mrs. Walter Jacobson,
New York, N.Y.

250. PEASANT'S HEAD / 1939 / Snakewood
Collection of Mr. Stephen Schwartz, New York, N.Y.

251. INNOCENCE / 1928 / Granidillo Wood
Collection of Mr. and Mrs. Walter Jacobson, New York, N.Y.

253. GUATEMALTECA / 1938 / Ebony
Collection of Mrs. Eda Cohn, Ossining, N.Y.

252. MADONNA / 1938 / Rosewood
Collection of Mr. and Mrs. Louis Friedenthal, New York, N.Y.

254. FEMME AU CHIGNON / 1932 / Walnut
Collection of the Artist (Courtesy of Kennedy Galleries)

255.   ABSTRACT / 1939 / Bois des Iles
Collection of Dr. Theodore J. Edlich, New York, N.Y.

256.   ABSTRACT FORM / 1961 / Walnut
Collection of Mr. and Mrs. George T. Delacorte, New York, N.Y.

257. L'ESCLAVE / 1922 / Bois d'Indochine
Collection of the Artist (Courtesy of Kennedy Galleries)

258. PORTRAIT OF MAX JIMENEZ / 1925 / Bois d'Orme
Collection of the Artist (Courtesy of Kennedy Galleries)

259. MYTHOLOGICAL CREATURES / 1927 /
French Pyrenees Marble
Collection of Mr. and Mrs. Robert Ward, Chicago, Ill.

260. LA PETITE PRINCESSE / 1939 / Green Porphyry
Collection of the Artist (Courtesy of Kennedy Galleries)

261–262. VOYAGE TO AFRICA / 1927 / Limestone
Collection of the Artist (Courtesy of Kennedy Galleries)

263.   BARBARE / 1915 / Bois de Chêne
Private Collection of the Artist

264.   LA FAMILLE / 1934 / Tulip Wood
Collection of Eva Campos

265. TUFF / 1940 / Red Pumice Stone
Private Collection of the Artist

266. CREATURE / 1927 / Chased Lead
Collection of the Artist (Courtesy of Kennedy Galleries)

267. FOUNTAIN / 1927–29 / Limestone
*Collection of Roberto Ramonje
at the Fortaleza of Majorca*

268. CAPITAL / 1927–29 / Limestone
Collection of Roberto Ramonje at the Fortaleza of Majorca

269. ENFANT ACROUPI / 1915 / Bois d'Indochine
Collection of Mr. and Mrs. William de Creeft, Homer, Alaska

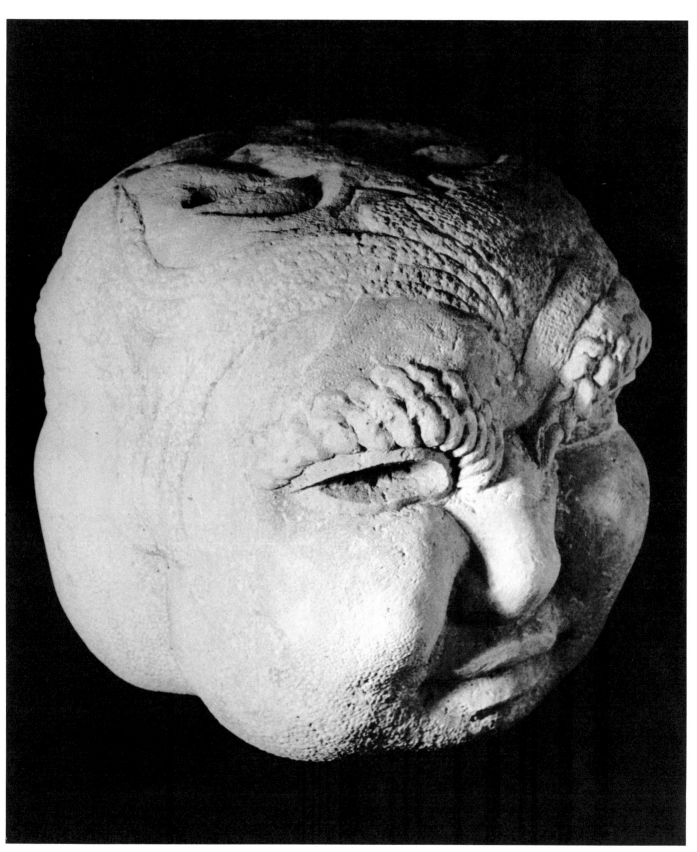

270. PHANTASY / 1940 / Sandstone
Collection of the Artist (Courtesy of Kennedy Galleries)

271. CAPITAL / 1927—29 / Limestone
Collection of Roberto Ramonje
at the Fortaleza of Majorca

272. CAPITAL / 1927—29 / Limestone
Collection of Roberto Ramonje
at the Fortaleza of Majorca

273. FOUNTAIN / 1927—29 / Limestone
Collection of Roberto Ramonje
at the Fortaleza of Majorca

274. FONTAINE / 1928 / Limestone
University of Puerto Rico, Rio Piedras, P.R.
Bronze: Collection of Mr. and Mrs. Abraham Feinberg,
Mt. Vernon, N.Y.

275. CRACHEUR D'EAU / 1926 / Limestone
Collection of Mr. Roberto Ramonje, Paris

276. FOUNTAIN / 1927 / Pink Bresche Marble
Collection of Roberto Ramonje at the Fortaleza of Majorca

277.   LE PICADOR / 1925 / Stove Pipe and Scrap Metal
Private Collection of the Artist

278.   OSTRICH / 1924 / Stove Pipe and Scrap Metal
Private Collection

279. THE FIFTH WHEEL / 1961 / Welded Metal
Collection of Shirley Sugarman, Summit, N.J.

280. BIRD / 1928 / Found Objects
Hirshhorn Museum and Sculpture Gardens, Smithsonian Institution

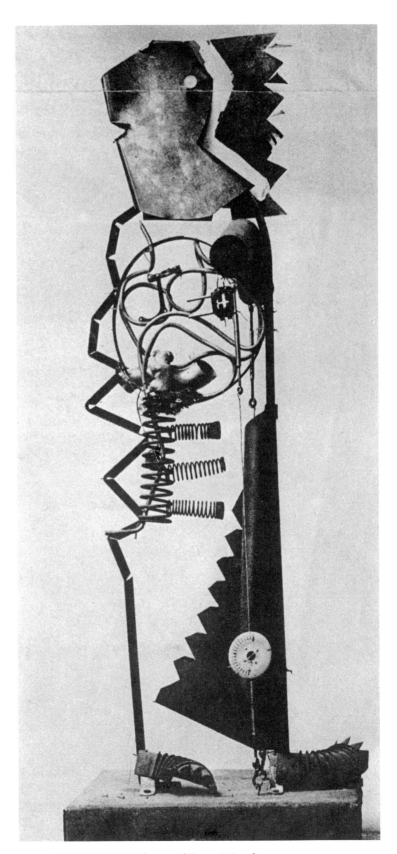

281.   MATERNITY / 1928 / Scrap Metal
Private Collection

282. ALICE IN WONDERLAND / 1959 / Bronze
Central Park, New York City (Dedicated in Memory of Marguerite Delacorte by the Delacorte Foundation)

283. NURSES / 1962 / Mosaic
Nurses' Residence and School, Bronx Municipal Hospital, Bronx, N.Y.

284.   THEME / 1958 / Hammered Copper
Jewish Community Center, White Plains, N.Y.

APPENDIX

BIOGRAPHICAL CHRONOLOGY

1884   Born November 27 in Guadalajara, Spain, of Catalan parents, Mariano and Rosa (Champane) de Creeft.

1888   Family moves to Barcelona.

1895   Makes first sculptures, crèches, which he fires in the oven at home and sells on the street near the Cathedral of Barcelona in competition with other children.

1897   Apprenticed in workshop of the religious *imagier*, Bernadas.

1898   Apprenticed at Masriera & Campins, bronze-art foundry.

1900   Family moves to Madrid. Apprenticed to Don Augustine Querol, official government sculptor. Also studies drawing with Idalgo de Caviedas.

1902   Takes first studio, located on the Calle Espanoletto, Madrid.

1903   First exhibition—clay and plaster portraits of children—El Circulo de Bellas Artes, Madrid.

1905   Moves to Paris. Takes studio in Batteau Lavoir, 13 rue de Ravignan, Montmartre. Begins formal art training at the Académie Julien.

1906   Awarded first prize, Concours de Sculpture, Académie Julien, for his *Torso*, executed in clay.

1909   Exhibits for the first time at the Salon des Artistes Français, Paris.

1911   Enters Maison Greber to learn traditional technique of reproducing sculpture in stone from clay and plaster models by use of the pointing machine (*mise aux points*).

1915   Rejects the *mise aux points* technique of making sculpture. Destroys all previous work in clay and plaster. Begins direct carving. Completes first carving in wood, *Barbare*.

1916   Completes first direct carving in stone, *Head* (red granite), which is exhibited at the Société Nationale des Beaux Arts. Also finishes first portrait carved from life, *Enigma* (black Belgian granite).

1917   Takes first private students.

[211]

1918   First major commission, *Le Poilu*, granite war memorial for Saugues (Puy de Dôme), France (completed 1921).

1919–
1928   Exhibits direct carvings in Paris at the Salon d'Automne, Salon des Tuileries, Salon des Artistes Indépendents, Société Nationale des Beaux Arts, Salon des Humoristes, Société d'Encouragement aux Arts.

1921   Executes twenty-one drawings for *Twenty-One Meditations*, a book by Albert Rid.

1925   Working spontaneously with stove pipe and scrap metal, creates *Le Picador*, an eight-foot-high figure on horseback. This piece is shown for the first time at a reception for the flamenco dancer, Escudero, and is exhibited in 1926 at the Salon des Artistes Indépendents.

1927–
1929   First major commission in Spain. In a period of eighteen months, completes two hundred direct carvings in stone for Roberto Ramonje's Forteleza of Majorca.

1929   In England in March, marries Alice Robertson Carr, sculptor from Roanoke, Virginia (divorced 1938). Comes to the United States in June. First one-man show in America, July, Seattle Art Institute. Visits West Coast, travels to New York City (September), takes studio at 1 Washington Place (the first of several New York studios). One-man show in December at Feragil Galleries.

1930   Using ball-peen hammers to make three-dimensional sculpture from flat sheets of lead—an innovative technique—creates *Portrait of Jolas* from life.

1931   Completes commissioned life-size portrait bust (beaten lead) of the actress Gertrude Lawrence. The work is first shown at the London opening of her play, *Can a Leopard?*

1932   Son William born. Accepts teaching position in scultpure, New School for Social Research, New York City.

1932–
1936   Travels intermittently to France and Spain. Takes groups of American students to Majorca for summer instruction, 1932 and 1936.

1933   Daughter Nina born.

1936   Joins Georgette Passedoit Gallery, New York City. Exhibits there through 1949.

1940   Becomes United States citizen.

1940–
1941   Fellowship, Yaddo, Saratoga Springs, N.Y. (Summers).

1944   Marries Lorrie Goulet, sculptor from Riverdale, New York. Spends summer as visiting instructor, Black Mountain College, North Carolina. Begins teaching at the Art Students League, New York City.

1948   Daughter Donna Maria born. Visiting instructor, Skowhegan (Maine) School of Painting and Sculpture (summer; also summer, 1949).

1948–
1951   Visiting instructor, Norton Gallery and School of Art, West Palm Beach, Florida (winters).

1951   First major American commission from Fairmount Park Association, Philadelphia: *Poet*, direct carving in granite, completed in 1956.

1956   Joins The Contemporaries (gallery], New York City. Remains through 1966.

1959   Awarded Ford Foundation traveling exhibition. Completes *Alice in Wonderland*, bronze group commissioned (1957) for Central Park, New York City.

1960   Retrospective exhibition at the Whitney Museum of American Art. Exhibition is subsequently circulated to thirteen other museums throughout the United States by the American Federation of Arts under the Ford Foundation award.

1962   Completes first work in mosaic, *Nurses*, commissioned (1961) by the City of New York for the Bronx Municipal Hospital.

1970   Joins the Kennedy Galleries, New York City.

MAJOR AWARDS AND HONORS

1923   Selected Officier de l'Instruction Publique, Paris.

1925   Represents Spain as jury member, International Exhibition, Paris.

1942   First Prize in Sculpture, *Artists for Victory*, Metropolitan Museum of Art (*Maternity*).

1945   George D. Widener Memorial Gold Medal, 140th Annual Exhibition, Pennsylvania Academy of Fine Arts, Philadelphia (*Rachmaninoff*).

1946   Elected Fellow, National Sculpture Society, New York City.

1954   Gold Medal, 12th Annual Exhibition, Audubon Artists, New York City (*Young Woman*).

1955   Elected to the National Institute of Arts and Letters.

1957   Medal of Honor, 15th Annual Exhibition, Audubon Artists, New York City (*Acrobat*).

1959   Awarded Ford Foundation Retrospective Traveling Exhibition.

1964   Elected Academician, National Academy of Design.

1969   Elected to the American Academy of Arts and Letters.

1969   Therese and Edwin H. Richard Memorial Prize, National Sculpture Society, New York City (*Dream*).

MEMBERSHIPS

American Academy of Arts and Letters

Artists Equity Association

Audubon Artists

Federation of Modern Painters and Sculptors

National Academy of Design

National Sculpture Society

Sculptors Guild

PUBLIC COMMISSIONS

1918   War Memorial, Saugues (Puy de Dôme), France: *Le Poilu* (granite); completed 1921.

1927– Two hundred sculptures in stone commissioned by Roberto Ramonje for the For-
1929   teleza of Majorca.

1951   Fairmount Park, Philadelphia: *Poet* (granite); completed 1956.

1957   Jewish Community Center, White Plains, New York: *Theme* (hammered copper); completed 1958.

1957   *Alice in Wonderland* (bronze group), commissioned by the Delacorte Foundation for Central Park, New York City; completed 1959.

1961   Nurses' Residence and School, Bronx Municipal Hospital, Bronx, New York: *Nurses* (mosaic mural); completed 1962.

1966   Public Health Laboratory, Bellevue Hospital, New York City: *Medical Science: The Gift of Health to Mankind* (bronze relief); completed 1967.

PUBLIC COLLECTIONS *(partial list)*

Art Students League, New York City

Bezalel Museum, Jerusalem, Israel
    (Billy Rose Collection)

Brooklyn Museum

Fairmount Park Art Association,
    Philadelphia

Hirshhorn Museum and Sculpture Gardens,
    Smithsonian Institution

Metropolitan Museum of Art

Munson-Williams-Proctor Institute,
    Utica, New York

Museum of Modern Art, New York City

Museum of the City of New York

New Jersey State Museum, Trenton

Norton Gallery of Art,
    West Palm Beach, Florida

Pennsylvania Academy of Fine Arts,
    Philadelphia

Roland T. Murdock Collection,
    Wichita Art Museum, Wichita, Kansas

Sarah Roby Foundation, New York City

Seattle Art Museum

Sheldon Art Gallery, University of Nebraska,
    Lincoln, Nebraska

Smithsonian Institution

State University of New York,
    New Paltz, New York

University of Puerto Rico,
    Rio Piedras, Puerto Rico

University of Tucson, Tucson, Arizona

Whitney Museum of American Art

ONE-MAN EXHIBITIONS

1929   Seattle (Washington) Art Institute
Feragil Galleries, New York City

1930   Arts Club of Chicago
Fifty-sixth Street Gallery, New York City

1932   Galleria Costa, Palma, Majorca

1933   Philadelphia Art Alliance
New School for Social Research, New York City (also 1934)

1936   Georgette Passedoit Gallery, New York City (also 1938, 1939, 1940, 1941, 1942, 1943, 1944, 1945, 1946, 1947, 1949)

1937   Faulkner Memorial Art Gallery, Santa Barbara, California

1943   St. Paul (Minnesota) Gallery and School of Art

1944   College of William and Mary, Williamsburg, Virginia

1949   Norton Gallery of Art, West Palm Beach, Florida

1956   The Contemporaries (gallery), New York City (also 1958, 1959, 1962, 1964, 1966)

1958   Southern Vermont Art Center, Manchester, Vermont

1960–1961   Ford Foundation Retrospective Traveling Exhibition circulated by the American Federation of Art:

1960

Whitney Museum of American Art (opened May 3)

State College of Indiana, Indiana, Pennsylvania

Allentown (Pennsylvania) Art Museum

Roberson Memorial Center, Binghampton, New York

Columbus (Ohio) Gallery of Fine Arts

Mint Museum of Art, Charlotte, North Carolina

1961

Florida State University, Tallahassee, Florida

Louisiana State University, Baton Rouge, Louisiana

Brooks Memorial Art Gallery, Memphis, Tennessee

Saginaw Museum, Saginaw, Michigan

Museum of Fine Arts, University of Virginia, Charlottesville, Virginia

Eastern Tennessee State College, Johnson City, Tennessee

University of Kentucky, Lexington, Kentucky

Howard University, Washington, D.C.

1962   Louis Alexander Gallery, New York City

1970   Kennedy Galleries, New York City (also 1971)

GROUP EXHIBITIONS *(partial list)*

1903   El Circulo de Bellas Artes, Madrid

1909   Salon des Artistes Francais, Paris (also 1910–1912, 1914)

1914   Société d'Encouragement aux Arts, Paris

1916   Société National des Beaux Arts, Paris (also 1918, 1920, 1927)

1919   Salon d'Automne, Paris (also 1920–1927, 1930)

1922   Salon des Artistes Indépendents, Paris (also 1923–1925, 1928)

1923   Salon des Tuileries, Paris (also 1925–1927, 1932)

1925   International Exhibition, Paris

1930   Brooklyn Museum (also 1936, 1944, 1966)
         Philadelphia Art Alliance (also 1933)

1932   Art Institute of Chicago (also 1935, 1939, 1951)

1933   New School for Social Research, New York City, *Annual* (also 1934–1939, 1957–1965)

1938   Sculptors Guild, New York City, *Annual* (also 1939, 1941, 1948, 1949, 1957, 1959, 1961, 1963, 1965, 1966)

1940   Philadelphia Museum of Art, *Sculpture Annual*

1939   Whitney Museum of American Art, *Annual* (also 1942–1944, 1946–1948, 1953, 1956, 1958)

1942   Metropolitan Museum of Art, *Artists for Victory* (other exhibitions 1952, 1958)
         National Academy of Design, New York City
         Pennsylvania Academy of Fine Arts, Philadelphia, *Annual* (also 1943–1947, 1952–1955, 1957, 1960, 1962, 1964)

1945   *Critic's Choice,* Seventeenth Regiment Armory, New York City

1947   Toledo Museum of Art, Toledo, Ohio, *Sculpture Today*

1949   Fairmount Park Art Association, Philadelphia, *International Art Show*
        Worcester Art Museum, Worcester Massachusetts, *Sculpture at the Crossroads*

1951   Museum of Modern Art, São Paulo, Brazil
        Munson-Williams-Proctor Institute, Utica, New York
        Audubon Artists, New York City, *Annual* (also 1953, 1954, 1956, 1957, 1962)

1953   Museum of Modern Art, New York City, *Sculpture of the 20th Century*

1958–   *God and Man in Art*, traveling exhibition organized by the American Federation of
1959   of Arts and shown at ten museums and institutions throughout the United States

1959   *Contemporary American Art*, organized by the Whitney Museum of American Art
        for exhibition in Moscow

        Art and the Found Object, exhibition circulated by the American Federation of Arts
        and shown at seven museums and institutions throughout the United States

1960   Detroit Institute of Fine Arts, *Second Biennial of American Painting and Sculpture*

1965   White House Festival of the Arts, Washington, D.C.

1967   Baltimore Museum of Art

SELECTED BIBLIOGRAPHY

"Addition v. Subtraction." *Time*, December 3, 1945, p. 67.

American Federation of Arts. *Sculpture in Silver.* Foreword by John Walker McCoubrey. New York: American Federation of Arts, 1955.

"Architectural Sculpture on Majorca." *Town & Country*, February 1, 1930, p. 70.

"Artists for Victory." *Magazine of Art*, January, 1943, p. 24.

"Artists for Victory Score Victory in Met." *Art Digest*, December 15, 1942, p. 5.

Baur, John I. H. *Contemporary Materials and Techniques in the Fine Arts.* Brooklyn: Brooklyn Museum, 1936.

"Ein Bildhauerscherz. Der Picador von José de Creeft." *Scherls Magazin* (Berlin), June, 1926, p. 560.

Boswell, Helen. "De Creeft's Three Assets." *Art Digest*, November 15, 1941, p. 23.

Campos, Jules. "Interview with de Creeft." *Liturgical Arts*, February, 1947, pp. 47–49.

Campos, Jules. *José de Creeft.* New York: Erich S. Herrmann, 1945.

"Carved by de Creeft." *Art Digest*, November 15, 1938, p. 21.

Chanin, A. L., *et al. Modern Art.* New York: Macmillan, 1959.

Cheney, Martha C. *Modern Art in America.* New York: Whittlesey House, 1939.

"Crowd of Climbers in Wonderland." *Life*, June 29, 1959, pp. 12–13.

Cunningham, John, ed. *José de Creeft.* American Sculptor's Series. Athens, Georgia: 1950.

Dame, Lawrence. "Sculpture at the Crossroads." *Art Digest*, March 1, 1948, p. 15.

Daniel, George. "José de Creeft." *New Masses*, January 1, 1946.

"De Creeft Carves Direct." *Look*, September 27, 1949, p. 13.

"De Creeft Continues His March to Fame." *Art Digest*, December 1, 1940, p. 12.

"De Creeft and His Rachmaninoff." *Newsweek*, December 6, 1943, p. 110.

"De Creeft, Vigorous, Versatile." *Art Digest*, January 1, 1936, p. 18.

Devree, Charlotte. *José de Creeft.* New York: American Federation of Arts, 1960.

Devree Howard. "New York Letter." *Magazine of Art*, April, 1941, p. 208.

————. "Sculpture Ascendant." *Magazine of Art*, February, 1939, p. 96.

"Four Sculptors." *Art Digest*, December 1, 1937, p. 19.

Frost, Rosamund. "First Sculptor from Spain." *Art News*, December 1, 1942, pp. 14–15.

————. "Sculptors on Park Avenue." *Art News*, April 16, 1938, p. 13.

Gomez-Gil, Alfredo. *Cerebros Españoles en U.S.A.* Barcelona: Plaza-Janes, S.A., 1971.

Grafly, Dorothy. "Interview with José de Creeft." *American Artist*, March, 1947, p. 30.

Goodrich, Lloyd, and Baur, John I. H. *American Art of Our Century.* New York: Praeger, 1961.

Jimenez, Max. "El Escultor José de Creeft." *Grafos* (Havana), December, 1935.

Landgren, Marchal. Review of *José de Creeft* by Jules Campos. *Magazine of Art*, December, 1946, p. 389.

Molé, Pierre. "Don Quichotte de de Creest [sic]." *Artistes d'Aujourd'hui*, April 15, 1926.

Munro, Eleanor. "Explorations in Form." *Perspectives U.S.A.*, Summer, 1956, pp. 160–172.

O'Hara, Eliot. "Portrait of de Creeft." *American Artist*, November, 1951, p. 30.

Pearson, Ralph M. *The Modern Renaissance in American Art*. New York: Harper, 1954.

"Recent Works by a Notable Sculptor." *Art News*, November 19, 1938, p. 15.

"Recognition for de Creeft." *Art Digest*, November 15, 1939, p. 18.

Reed, Judith K. Review of *José de Creeft* by Jules Campos. *Art Digest*, March 1, 1946, p. 24.

Rich, Jack C. *The Materials and Methods of Sculpture*. New York: Oxford University Press, 1947.

Riley, Maude. "Carved by de Creeft." *Art Digest*, December 1, 1944, p. 10.

_____. "Portrays Rachmaninoff in Lead." *Art Digest*, December 1, 1943, p. 16.

Ritchie, Andrew C. *Sculpture of the Twentieth Century*. New York: Museum of Modern Art, 1952.

"Le Salon des Indépendants 1926." *L'Art Vivant* (Paris), April 1, 1926.

Schnier, Jacques P. *Sculpture in Modern America*. Berkeley: University of California Press, 1948.

Schwartz, M. "Portrait of de Creeft." *Art News*, June, 1942, p. 21.

Selz, Jean. *Modern Sculpture: Origins and Evolution*. Trans. Annette Michelson. New York: Braziller, 1963.

"Shockless Sculptor." *Time*, December 16, 1929, p. 37.

"A Spaniard." *Art Digest*, December 1, 1929, p. 19.

"Symposium: The Creative Process." *Art Digest*, January 15, 1954, p. 14.

"Three American Artists." *Vogue*, October 15, 1957, p. 78.

Wellman, Rita. "A Sculptor in Unusual Medium." *Home & Field*, February, 1930, p. 58.

Welty, Eudora. "José de Creeft." *Magazine of Art*, February, 1944, pp. 42–47.

Wolf, Ben. "Monumental, Compelling Work of de Creeft." *Art Digest*, December 1, 1945, p. 11.

"The Year in Art—Ten Best of 1942." *Art News*, January 1, 1943, p. 24.

"The Year in Art—Ten Best of 1944." *Art News*, January 1, 1945, p. 27.

Verburgh, Medard. "Portrait of de Creeft." *Art Digest*, January 1, 1931, p. 13.

Zegri, Armando. "The Spanish Sculptor José de Creeft." *Alhambra*, January, 1930, pp. 12–13.

Zorach, William. "American Sculpture." *Studio* (London), June, 1944, p. 187.

INDEX OF ILLUSTRATIONS

[224]

PICTURE CREDITS